W9-AQY-145

# MODERN NOVELISTS

General Editor: Norman Page

# MODERN NOVELISTS

*Published titles*

ALBERT CAMUS   Philip Thody
FYODOR DOSTOEVSKY   Peter Conradi
WILLIAM FAULKNER   David Dowling
GUSTAVE FLAUBERT   David Roe
E. M. FORSTER   Norman Page
WILLIAM GOLDING   James Gindin
GRAHAM GREENE   Neil McEwan
CHRISTOPHER ISHERWOOD   Stephen Wade
HENRY JAMES   Alan Bellringer
D. H. LAWRENCE   G. M. Hyde
DORIS LESSING   Ruth Whittaker
MALCOLM LOWRY   Tony Bareham
THOMAS MANN   Martin Travers
GEORGE ORWELL   Valerie Meyers
ANTHONY POWELL   Neil McEwan
MARCEL PROUST   Philip Thody
BARBARA PYM   Michael Cotsell
SIX WOMEN NOVELISTS   Merryn Williams
MURIEL SPARK   Norman Page
JOHN UPDIKE   Judie Newman
EVELYN WAUGH   Jacqueline McDonnell
H. G. WELLS   Michael Draper
VIRGINIA WOOLF   Edward Bishop

*Forthcoming titles*

MARGARET ATWOOD   Coral Ann Howells
SAUL BELLOW   Paul Hyland
IVY COMPTON-BURNETT   Janet Godden
JOSEPH CONRAD   Owen Knowles
GEORGE ELIOT   Alan Bellringer
F. SCOTT FITZGERALD   John Whitley
JOHN FOWLES   James Acheson
ERNEST HEMINGWAY   Peter Messent
JAMES JOYCE   Richard Brown
NORMAN MAILER   Michael Glenday
V. S. NAIPAUL   Bruce King
PAUL SCOTT   G. K. Das
PATRICK WHITE   Mark Williams

MODERN NOVELISTS

# THOMAS MANN

Martin Travers

St. Martin's Press      New York

First published in the United States of America in 1992

Printed in Hong Kong

ISBN 0–312–07206–6

Library of Congress Cataloging-in-Publication Data
Travers, Martin Patrick Anthony.
Thomas Mann / Martin Travers.
p.   cm. — (Modern novelists)
Includes bibliographical references and index.
ISBN 0–312–07206–6
1. Mann, Thomas, 1875–1955—Criticism and interpretation.
I. Title.   II. Series.
PT2625.A44Z922147   1992
833'.912—dc20                                    91–31847
                                                       CIP

# Contents

# General Editor's Preface

The death of the novel has often been announced, and part of the secret of its obstinate vitality must be its capacity for growth, adaptation, self-renewal and self-transformation: like some vigorous organism in a speeded-up Darwinian ecosystem, it adapts itself quickly to a changing world. War and revolution, economic crisis and social change, radically new ideologies such as Marxism and Freudianism, have made this century unprecedented in human history in the speed and extent of change, but the novel has shown an extraordinary capacity to find new forms and techniques and to accommodate new ideas and conceptions of human nature and human experience, and even to take up new positions on the nature of fiction itself.

In the generations immediately preceding and following 1914, the novel underwent a radical redefinition of its nature and possibilities. The present series of monographs is devoted to the novelists who created the modern novel and to those who in their turn, either continued and extended, or reacted against and rejected, the traditions established during that period of intense exploration and experiment. It includes a number of those who lived and wrote in the nineteenth century but whose innovative contribution to the art of fiction makes it impossible to ignore them in any account of the origins of the modern novel; it also includes the so-called 'modernists' and those who in the mid- and late twentieth century have emerged as outstanding practitioners of this genre. The scope is, inevitably, international; not only, in the migratory and exile-haunted world of our century, do writers refuse to heed national frontiers – 'English' literature lays claim to Conrad the Pole, Henry James the American, and Joyce the Irishman – but geniuses such as Flaubert, Dostoevsky and Kafka have had an influence on the fiction of many nations.

Each volume in the series is intended to provide an introduction to the fiction of the writer concerned, both for those
approaching him or her for the first time and for those who are
already familiar with some parts of the achievement in question
and now wish to place it in the context of the total *oeuvre*.
Although essential information relating to the writer's life and
times is given, usually in an opening chapter, the approach is
primarily critical and the emphasis is not upon 'background' or
generalisations but upon close examination of important texts.
Where an author is notably prolific, major texts have been made
to convey, more summarily, a sense of the nature and quality of
the author's work as a whole. Those who want to read further
will find suggestions in the select bibliography included in each
volume. Many novelists are, of course, not only novelists but also
poets, essayists, biographers, dramatists, travel writers and so
forth; many have practised shorter forms of fiction; and many
have written letters or kept diaries that constitute a significant
part of their literary output. A brief study cannot hope to deal
with all these in detail, but where the shorter fiction and the
non-fictional writings, public and private, have an important
relationship to the novels, some space has been devoted to them.

NORMAN PAGE

For Ann, 'il miglior fabbro'

# 1

# Thomas Mann: Between Patrician and Artist

In 1930, Thomas Mann published his only autobiography. Entitled *Lebensabriß (Sketch of My Life)*, this memoir encompassed the major events of Mann's life, from his birth in Lübeck in 1875 to his acceptance of the Nobel Prize for Literature in 1929. Mann was at this time at the height of his literary career and reputation, and he viewed the latter event as the culmination of a life's work that had begun over a quarter of a century earlier. After the exertions of a life dedicated to art, he had, he felt, been rightly called into the 'circle of the immortals', to join the great names of European literature.[1] It is easy to understand why Mann should depict himself in this rather grandiose manner. From his first (and most popular) novel, *Buddenbrooks*, through such masterpieces as *Death in Venice* and *The Magic Mountain*, his work had withstood the changing literary fashions of an era in which the nineteenth-century style of Realism had given way to the more intense and inward-looking movement of Expressionism, and which in turn had come to be replaced in the 1930s by a literature of political engagement. For a reading public bewildered and distressed by the disruptive energies and tensions of the modern world, Mann came increasingly to be regarded as a figure of patrician strength, as someone who, detached from the crises of his times, stood for continuity rather than crisis, moderation rather than excess.

This image of Mann as an Olympian author obscures, however, more than it reveals of the artist who existed behind the public persona. Both his life and art evolved around the claims of two competing identities: on the one hand, the conservative patrician figure whose roots were in the nineteenth-century

1

*Bildungsbürgertum* (educated bourgeoisie), and, on the other, a
private self, highly self-conscious and given to introversion, that
periodically questioned the very nature and validity of writing as
a vocation. This tension can also be seen in Mann's work, which
likewise underwent vital and quite varied changes from the
serious and 'death-sympathetic' works of *Death in Venice* and
*The Magic Mountain* to the more humorous and 'life-affirming'
writing of *Royal Highness* and *Lotte in Weimar*, from the charm-
ingly domestic vignettes of 'A Man and his Dog' to the epic
confrontation with German history depicted in *Doctor Faustus*.
Likewise in his own life, Mann went through a number of
personal, philosophical and political crises, and was only too
aware that the solid patrician image that he had acquired in the
minds of the public owed as much to fiction as it did to reality. It
is, however, precisely this duality in his life and art, this tension
between the outward-looking patrician and the inward-looking
artist, that bestows upon Mann's work a distinctly modern
dimension and makes him one of the great representative
authors of the modern period.

Thomas Mann was born, as Paul Thomas Mann, in Lübeck,
on the North German coast, on 6 June 1875. Since the founding
of the Hanseatic League in the twelfth century, Lübeck had been
an outlet for the large grain-producing areas of the Baltic
regions, and it was as traders in wheat that the Mann family had
earned a solid and respected position in Lübeck society. Mann's
father, Thomas Johann Heinrich, born in 1840, continued in this
tradition, and, in appreciation of his contributions to the community, was made a senator of his native city in 1877. Mann's
father was the epitome of patrician values, a figure of solid
achievement, of dignity and acumen, who continued to exercise
a decisive influence on his son long after his death.[2]

His mother, however, was of quite a different temperament.
She was born in 1851 as Julia da Silva-Bruhns, the daughter of a
Brazilian plantation owner, Johann Ludwig Bruhns, himself an
erstwhile native of Lübeck. Thomas Mann's mother was, according to her contemporaries, of exceptional beauty and musically
gifted. She was, in many ways, a positive antithesis to the solid
citizen and businessman who was her husband. Thomas Mann
liked to think of this marriage as a fruitful harmony of opposite
temperaments, whose union was reflected in the dual nature of
his own personality: 'When I ask myself about the hereditary

origin of my characteristics, I am fain to recall Goethe's famous little verse, and say too that I have from my father "the propensity to lead a serious life", but from my mother "the sunny nature", the sensuous artistic side, and in the wider sense the "tendency to fabulate" '.[3] This dichotomy between the rational, sensible North and the irrational, temperamental South, between action and introspection, commerce and art was to emerge as a major theme in much of his later fiction.

In spite of these radical differences of temperament, the marriage seems to have been successful. Three girls were born and two boys: Thomas and his elder brother, Heinrich, who also became a major writer. Thomas attended school between 1882 and 1889 without achieving conspicuous academic success, but developing a taste for amateur dramatics and literature, and establishing a journal of the arts, the *Frühlingssturm (Spring Storm)*, which provided a short-lived vehicle for his youthful literary efforts. The idyll of these years was violently interrupted in 1891 by the sudden death of his father, at the age of 51, from blood poisoning. The shock was more than just a personal one, for it transpired that the company of which his father had been the paternal head had long been in financial decline and, with the death of Johann Mann, it went into liquidation. For the Mann family, it meant the end of a way of life.

The financial crisis in the Mann family necessitated a move from Lübeck, and the acquisition of gainful employment for the sons. In 1894, Thomas found a position as clerk in an insurance company in Munich where the family had settled. This position was to last a mere six months; he resigned in the autumn of the same year, ostensibly to undertake studies at the *Technische Hochschule* (Technical University) with a view to becoming a journalist. But the real reason for this shift in professional emphasis lay in the publication of his first short story, 'Die Gefallen' ('The Fallen'), earlier in the year. On the basis of the success of that publication, and helped by a small annual endowment from his mother, Thomas went to Italy to join his brother Heinrich, who was already beginning to make a career for himself as a writer. It was in Italy that Thomas continued to write short stories, publishing 'Disillusionment', 'The Dilettante' and 'Little Herr Friedemann', in the following two years. It was on his second visit to Italy in 1887 that he started work on his first novel, *Buddenbrooks*. Subtitled 'The Decline of a Family', the

novel depicts the decline of an old merchant family, which
founders because it is unable to come to terms with the new
capitalist ethos of the period. The novel draws much of its
emotional and psychological appeal from the fact that its origins
are entirely autobiographical: Mann was reading the fate of his
own family in heroic-tragic terms, presenting it as symbolic of
the end of an era and of an entire social class, the cultured
bourgeoisie.

Although *Buddenbrooks* was eventually to become Mann's
most popular work, success did not come overnight. As Mann's
publisher, Samuel Fischer, had noted on receiving the manu-
script, the sheer length of the novel discouraged its immediate
readership, and its large-scale acceptance had to wait until a less
costly single volume edition appeared in 1904. But the literary
cognoscenti of pre-war Munich did recognize its status as a
major novel of social mores. With the success of *Buddenbrooks*,
Mann was soon able to become a full-time writer. His first book
of short-stories had appeared in 1898, and a second volume
*Tristan* in 1903. Mann now began to cultivate the image of the
'author', viewing himself as a figure of some importance in the
eclectic world of German *belles-lettres*. In an introduction to one
of the short stories of this period, he found a sufficiently theatrical
metaphor for his new identity: 'I am no longer sitting in my little
room alone, free and without obligations, creating art for art's
sake. I feel as though I have fallen within range of an immense
spotlight, which has made me visible to the public eye and that I
am now burdened with the responsibility of using my talents
which I have been foolish enough to reveal to others'.[4]

It was on the basis of his reputation as a new and up-and-
coming artist that Mann gained entry into the exclusive cultural
circles of the Munich *Bildungsbürgertum* (the cultured
bourgeoisie), which included the household of the Professor for
Mathematics at Munich University, Alfred Pringsheim. The
Pringsheim home presented Mann with the spectacle of a cultivated environment, with which he had not been familiar since
the dark days of the dissolution of his own home in 1891. As he
later noted: 'The atmosphere of the Pringsheim home, that great
family house that recalled my own early abode, enchanted me. I
had known the traditional elegance that belonged to the great
families; here I found it transformed and intellectualized in this
stately society compact of art and literature'.[5] It was here that

Mann met his future wife, the youngest daughter of the household, Katja, whom he married in 1905.

Mann had by now become a part of the social and cultural
establishment of pre-First World War Munich, and much of his
time during these early years of his marriage was spent on
lecture tours. He was also the head of a solid and ever-growing
family. The first child, Erika, was born in November 1905 and
she was followed over a period of thirteen years by a further four
children. This sense of belonging, of being a part of the establishment, a supporter of the values of the family and society, finds
expression in Mann's second novel of this period, *Royal Highness*, published in 1909. Perhaps because Mann had banished
the element of tragedy from his world and replaced it with
optimism, or because the novel takes place almost in a fairy-tale
world, and in a fairy-tale time, and hence lacks the solidity of
theme and characterization that supported the epic realism of
*Buddenbrooks*, for whatever reason *Royal Highness* was a success
neither with the critics nor the public.

The completion of *Royal Highness* was soon followed by work
on a third novel: *The Confessions of Felix Krull, Confidence Man*.
But *Krull*, like the subsequent short story that was to be *The
Magic Mountain*, was left unfinished. This hiatus in Mann's
writing was not overcome until 1911, when he returned to a
more personal theme to take stock, once again, of his life, and to
speculate upon the artistic direction that he seemed to be taking.
The result of this process of self-enquiry was the dramatically
original novella, *Death in Venice*. In the story, Mann seems to be
taking stock of certain proclivities within himself: artistic and
sexual. The theme of the artist who has sacrificed his commitment to psychological insight in his writings in order to maintain
a safe public image clearly reflects the strained optimism of the
period that saw the writing of *Royal Highness*. And even the
homo-erotic dimension of the story, Aschenbach's infatuation
with Tadzio, the boy transfigured into a Greek god, has its
origins in the ambiguous nature of Mann's own sexuality, which,
in his days as student and bohemian artist, led him into an
infatuation with certain of his young male friends.[6]

*Death in Venice* deals with a controversial theme, and Mann
expected its publication to cause a furore. The fact that it did not
can be explained by the growing acceptance among the reading
public of new thinking on sexuality, a thinking produced both by

creative writers such as Frank Wedekind, and by theorists such as Sigmund Freud. It also owed a great deal to the fact that German society had more to worry about than the amorous regard of an ageing artist for a young boy, as that nation and Europe stumbled from one minor crisis to another, in an inexorable movement towards the ultimate catastrophe of the First World War.

The outbreak of the First World War in August 1914 found Thomas Mann at the height of his artistic and personal acclaim. The growing popularity of his work meant that the 39 year-old writer was able to build a second home, a town house in a fashionable suburb of Munich. With the occupancy of certain official offices within the Bavarian State, invitations from foreign countries and a growing body of friends and admirers, Mann could rightly be seen as one of the pillars of the cultural establishment of Wilhelminian Germany. Within this context, Mann's response to the outbreak of war in August 1914 was, perhaps, predictable. As he wrote to Richard Dehmel in December of that year, the noted author was ready 'to put [his] mind, at least, directly in the service of the German cause'.[7] Over a period of several months, he composed a number of essays defending the German mobilization against criticisms made both outside of Germany and, more importantly, from within. In such essays as 'Thoughts in a Time of War' and 'Frederick and the Grand Coalition', Mann, for the first time, moves away from his earlier purely literary identity to adopt an explicitly *political* voice.

Although he was later to typify his writings on the war as the reflections of a 'nonpolitical man', these early jingoistic essays brought Mann firmly into the nationalist camp. They also led to a bitter split with his brother, Heinrich. A certain amount of tension had already existed between the two brothers prior to 1914, caused principally by divergences of life-style between the settled bourgeois and civically-minded Thomas, and the bohemian and free-living Heinrich. But the differences were also political; as Thomas seemed intent on ignoring the shortcomings of his contemporary society, where (according to Heinrich) all political power resided in the hands of Junkers, large industrialists and the Army, the elder brother was becoming increasingly more radical, and largely as the result of his contact with the more cosmopolitan and socially conscious traditions of the literature of France (a country now at war with Germany). The result of this newly-found political perspective was the novel *The Man of Straw*, written just before the outbreak of war, in which the prejudices, small town mentality and grovelling adulation for authority amongst the German middle-classes were mercilessly caricatured. In its clear rejection of the values of the status quo, Heinrich's novel stood in sharp contrast to the celebration of such values in Thomas's *Royal Highness*.[8]

The events of the First World War brought to a head, then, rather than produced the differences between the two brothers. The immediate occasion of the breach was an essay published by Heinrich on the subject of one of his favourite French authors, the Naturalist writer Emile Zola. Simply entitled 'Zola', the essay was on the surface purely a review in the form of a short biography of the achievements of that author. But in its emphasis upon Zola's social conscience, his readiness to defend the down-trodden and persecuted and his critical stance towards his own society (which included a pacifist worldview), Heinrich Mann's character portrait of his hero stood (and was meant to stand) in sharp contrast to those writers who either ignored political matters entirely, or put their pens to the service of their countries, even to the point of justifying a clearly aggressive war.

Thomas Mann saw the essay as a challenge to his patriotic values *and* to his role as a writer and artist. Meeting this challenge took Mann the greater part of the war, and resulted in the most extensive formulation of his political, moral and artistic credo: *The Reflections of a Nonpolitical Man*. Described by Mann himself as the result of a period of 'thrashing through a pathless underbrush' of ideas, *The Reflections* constitutes a loosely-knit body of comments upon German culture, 'something intermediate between work and effusion, composition and hackwork'.[9] Its central argument is that German *Kultur* possesses a unique character which makes it unsuitable for the type of democratic politics favoured in France and England. Through heavy-handed allusions, Mann made it quite clear that writers such as his brother Heinrich, whom he termed a *Zivilisationsliterat* (a 'literary dilettante') were more sociologists than artists, incapable of appreciating the intangible and the spiritual side of life. Without a sense for the mystery of tradition and 'culture' (which could not be grasped by the sort of pragmatic rationalism that was so prized in the barren 'civilization' of the

West), such scribblers could not (Mann argued) see that the
Germans were fighting the war not for the sake of property and
territory, but so that certain German *values* might be retained.

The publication of *The Reflections* in 1918 made Thomas
Mann many friends within conservative circles, but it is doubtful
whether the targets of Mann's ire would have had the opportunity of becoming outraged by his lengthy tirades. Within a week of
the book's publication, the war lost and Kaiser abdicated,
Germany found itself on the brink of revolution and civil war.
The Mann family, isolated in Munich, the scene of the short-
lived Workers' Republic in 1919, survived as best they could. It
was time for Mann to retire from the political scene, and devote
himself to his writings and his family. Two further children were
born (Elizabeth in 1918 and Michael in 1919), further short
stories completed and work resumed on a piece of literature that
had begun life before the war as an intended short story but now
was to become Mann's major novel of the inter-war years: *The
Magic Mountain*. At the same time, Mann resumed his routine of
lecture tours, speeches, book reviews and other tasks in an
attempt to keep himself and family afloat in the years of rampant
inflation that immediately followed the end to the revolutionary
turmoil. As the prospect of a Communist revolution in Germany
decreased and a parliamentary democracy along Western lines
came to be installed, Mann soon found that his position and
status in the new Weimar Republic was as solid as it had been in
Imperial Germany. He came, accordingly, to abandon his previously negative views on Western liberalism, and entered his
second political phase, characterized by a growing commitment
to democracy and democratic socialism, which he defended
against attacks from the increasingly hysterical agitators for a
resurgent nationalism.

Mann's political change of heart was consolidated by a rap-
prochement with his brother Heinrich in 1922, which laid the
basis for fraternal co-operation that was to last for the rest of
their lives. In the same year, Mann produced his major testimony to this new political direction: the speech 'Von deutscher
Republik' ('The German Republic'). Shocked by the violence
perpetrated by nationally-minded youth, Mann argued that true
German culture was humanist not reactionary in nature, and
required a sound democratic state for its realization. The speech
represents, in many ways, a form of self-criticism, for (as many of

his conservative friends and supporters reluctantly noted) it contradicted many of the ideas expressed in *The Reflections of a Nonpolitical Man*, published a mere four years before. But Mann had seen the ominous path that nationalist politics was taking, and had recognized the nihilism that lay behind its apparent idealism.

His next novel, *The Magic Mountain*, was published soon after, in 1924. It was a novel which, in its setting and intellectual ambit, could claim to be Mann's first truly European work. Its publication and translation into English (in 1927) and French (in 1931) opened up contacts and cultural ties throughout America and Europe, particularly with France, which he visited in 1926. At home and abroad, Mann came to be recognized as one of the pre-eminent novelists of his generation, and his help was enlisted in the founding of the literary section of the Prussian Academy of the Arts in 1928. Finally, in 1929 Mann became the first German writer for seventeen years to receive the Nobel Prize for literature.

Fame served to increase Mann's representative status in the eyes of the public, but at the same time it increased his importance as a target for his political enemies, particularly those amongst the increasingly vociferous radical Right. In an article published in 1927, Mann was accused of kowtowing to France and serving the interests of 'international Jewry'. Such a scurrilous character assassination could be easily death with, both because it was itself untrue, but also because it emanated from the pens of a small if noisy minority of political fanatics.[10] The danger increased dramatically, however, in 1930, when, in the general election of that year, the Nazi Party under Adolf Hitler succeeded for the first time in gaining large popular support. Horrified by their successes and dismayed by the fact that the Nazi Party had apparently attracted large numbers of middle-class voters who had previously been of a moderately conservative disposition, Mann re-entered the political arena. In his speech, significantly entitled 'A German Address: a Call to Reason', given in Berlin in 1930, Mann warned his audience against the radical solutions and panaceas advanced by the Nazi Party to deal with the social and economic problems besetting a strife-torn Germany. On the surface, the National Socialists seemed to represent a new idealism and rebirth of national pride, but their rhetoric hid a cynical power-centred politics that

*Thomas Mann*

had a further European war and world domination as its real agenda.

Mann had tried to give literary form to a similar message the year before in his short story, 'Mario and the Magician'. There he had shown how difficult it is to resist the charismatic attraction of a powerful personality, unless the individual has a set of firm beliefs; simply saying 'no' is not enough: 'Between not willing a certain thing and not willing at all – in other words, yielding to another person's will – there may lie too small a space for the idea of freedom to squeeze into'.[11]

It was the need to find a set of humane values sufficiently powerful to set against the nihilistic direction of the times that inspired Mann to start work on a project that was to take him fifteen years to complete: the novel tetralogy *Joseph and His Brothers*. Begun in 1926, the Joseph novel takes as its starting point the Biblical story of Joseph's adventures in Egypt. In Mann's hands, the story became a medium in which the founding values of Judaic-Christian humanism could be used as the basis for a critique of the fanaticism and chauvinism that he saw around him in his contemporary world. The novel also provided Mann with a point of personal stability and sustenance, as events in the political world of his contemporary Germany deteriorated rapidly. Hitler was able to consolidate his early victory in 1930 with a 'seizure of power' in 1933. Mann's warnings had gone unheeded. In March of that year, he left for a lecture tour of Holland and France, and was not to see Germany again for fourteen years. Mann was about to enter the third phase in his life, a period of exile, of suffering and disorientation, from which he would only slowly recover.

Thomas Mann's period of exile began in Switzerland, where, in Küsnacht, near Zurich, he took up residence after a short stay in France in September, 1933. Unlike many writers known for their liberal and democratic inclinations, including his brother Heinrich, Mann had not been officially blacklisted by the new Nazi regime in Germany, nor had his works been consigned to the flames in the infamous book-burning of May of that year. Nevertheless, his numerous attestations of faith in the Weimar Republic and his abhorrence of National Socialism were still vivid in the minds of Nazi politicians, and Mann suffered as a consequence. The Munich family home and its contents were confiscated, and it was made clear to him that his personal safety would be in jeopardy were he to return to the country.

The severing of ties with Germany caused Mann much emotional distress. 'I am much too good a German', he wrote to his Italian translator in early 1933, 'far too closely linked with the cultural traditions and the language of my country, for the thought of an exile lasting years, if not a full life time, not to have a grave, a fateful significance to me'.[12] It was, above all, his reading public that Mann most feared losing, not only because that would have entailed dire financial consequences through loss of royalties, but (and more importantly) because without a public he would have been writing in a vacuum. The problem was at least partially solved by his publisher, Gottfried Bermann-Fischer, who was able to reach a compromise with the authorities in Germany, and continue publishing Mann's works, including the first volume of the Joseph tetralogy, *The Tales of Jacob*, which appeared in 1933. As he wrote in his diary at the time, Mann tried to find a middle way 'between the often hysterical outrage of the emigré journalists and the supine attitude of authors ready to cooperate in the "reconstruction"'.[13] It was not an ideal situation. Going along with this arrangement gave the impression to the ever growing emigré community, many of whom were experiencing severe hardship, that Mann was colluding with the system. There is, indeed, a certain substance in this view, for Mann, at least in public, was forced to refrain from espousing the emigré cause, and to desist from explicit political denunciations of the Nazi regime. He was careful, for example, to distance himself from the policies advocated by the anti-Nazi emigré journal, *Die Sammlung*, founded by his son, Klaus, in 1933. Thomas Mann was in a double-bind, and his awareness of this dilemma, together with other pressures imposed by the material circumstances of his exile, produced in him a 'state of weariness, spiritual weakness and ennui' that seriously hampered his writing.[14] These were not productive years for Mann, as he slowly and painfully progressed on the third volume of his Joseph novel.

The situation changed dramatically in 1936, as it ultimately had to. Mann had long been under pressure to clarify and make public his position on the Nazi regime, and this he finally did in February of that year in an open letter to the features' editor of the *Neue Züricher Zeitung*, Eduard Korradi, who had maintained that Mann was not a part of the emigré movement (which he mischievously characterized as being entirely of Jewish extraction). Mann replied with an unequivocal denunciation of Nazi Germany and all it stood for. It was the final step for both parties; within twelve months the Nazi Government had revoked Mann's citizenship, placed his books on the black list and instructed the University of Bonn to withdraw his honorary doctorate. The decision of the Nazi authorities simplified the options open to Mann, and he greeted them with a sense of liberation. He was now able to embrace the emigré cause in an open and forceful manner, launching himself into a sustained campaign of writing aimed at unmasking the warlike aspirations of the Nazi State and warning Europe of its menace. In essays such as 'Mass und Wert' ('Measure and Value') (1937), 'The Coming Victory of Democracy' (1938), 'A Brother' (1939) and 'The Problem of Freedom' (1939), he combined a sense of moral outrage against the barbarism of the Hitler regime with an increasing acumen for political analysis. Such writings were of enormous significance to emigré organizations and individuals, and useful texts in what had by now crystallized into the European movement of the Popular Front against Fascism. Mann made a further contribution to this cause by co-founding the journal *Mass und Wert* in 1937, which was intended as a forum for the best humanistic writing of the era.

But writing alone could not stop Hitler. In recognition of the growing threat posed by Germany, which had exercised its military muscles in re-occupying the Rhineland in 1936 and annexing Austria in 1938, Mann decided to move himself and his family from Switzerland to America in 1938, whilst he was on his fourth lecture tour of that country. For the first time in this period of exile, he was provided with financial support and a professional livelihood, first as lecturer at Princeton University, then as consultant at the Library of Congress in Washington. America also provided Mann with personal and emotional security, since not only had many of his German friends and colleagues, such as Franz Werfel, Erich Kahler, Bruno Walter and Bruno Frank, emigrated to America at about the same time; but he discovered that his works in English translation had won an enthusiastic American readership, and he found himself fêted by a public that included the President of the United States, Franklin D. Roosevelt. It was in this context that Mann was able to complete his novel *Lotte in Weimar* in 1939, the final volume of his Joseph novel, *Joseph the Provider* in 1943, and to start work on *Doctor Faustus*.

Writing towards the end of his life, Thomas Mann was to regret that he did not conclude his life's work with the publication of *Doctor Faustus* in 1947.[15] It is easy to understand such a sentiment. The novel takes up and reworks many of the themes of Mann's earlier fiction: the conflict between the amoral artist and society, the proximity between sickness and knowledge and the longing for transcendence that characterized the *fin de siècle* generation. It treats such themes, however, within the broad historical context of the crisis of European politics brought about by Hitler's drive for world power. *Doctor Faustus* is also a highly personal novel, because it views the power philosophy of Hitlerism as an emanation of a specifically *German* psyche, as the logical culmination of the cultural and intellectual development of the nation of which Mann, in spite of his American citizenship, was still very much a part.

The genesis of the novel, which was later to be reconstructed by Mann himself in the autobiographical account, *The Story of a Novel*, lies in his attempts to explain to himself and others how Hitler could have won so much popular support (and from all sections of society) for his nihilistic war aims. Mann had grappled with this problem before in essays such as 'Schicksal und Aufgabe' ('War and the Future') (1944) and 'Deutschland und die Deutschen' ('Germany and the Germans') (1945), in which Germany (like the character Faust himself) is seen as a nation which combines good and evil, the moral and the amoral, the rational and the irrational in an inextricable way. This pessimistic and somewhat fatalistic interpretation of the German psyche necessarily brought Mann into conflict with other members of the emigré movement in America, notably Bertolt Brecht, who, through the organization Council for a Democratic Germany, wished to help reconstruct the defeated Germany on the basis of the 'good' elements who had stayed behind to offer opposition to Hitler in the German resistance movement. Mann came close to joining this organization in 1943, but backed away, not only because he discovered that it was largely run by communists and their sympathizers, but because he could not accept one of the tenets of the organization: that the German people had been led into the war by a minority of fanatics and, hence, were largely innocent of the crimes committed under the banner of National Socialism. Mann's response was to inscribe the predicament of German history into his novel *Doctor Faustus*, rather than offer political solutions.

The cessation of hostilities in 1945 should have meant the end of exile, and the beginning of a period of retirement for the 70 year-old Mann. Calls from the defeated Germany that he should return were numerous, including one from an erstwhile member of the Prussian Academy of Arts, Walter von Molo; but the memories of the early days of exile were too alive for a return to Germany to be contemplated. Above all, he could not believe that those who had remained behind in Hitler's Germany, even if they had chosen so-called 'inner emigration', had not been tainted by the odour of corruption that had pervaded the land under Hitler.[16] Mann could not, therefore, go back; but he also could not stay. The country that had shown such openness and largesse of spirit to the emigrés earlier in the war was now in the grip of Macarthyism, an anti-communist fever that was twisting minds that had previously been open and tolerant. Even passing references made by Mann in his writings and speeches to the need to establish a fairer and more socially just European state were interpreted as signs of support for 'world communism'. Such hysterical, irrational and blind hatred was all too reminiscent of Nazi Germany.

Thomas Mann left America with his wife for the last time in 1952, to take up residency once again in Switzerland. There was, understandably, a sense of finality about this move, inaugurating, as it did, the last stage in Mann's life. Death was coming ever closer to him, not just in the form of his own severe illnesses, but through the loss of two members of the family: his son, Klaus (through suicide) in 1949, and his brother, Heinrich, in 1950. According to his own accounts, these last years find him listless and without energy, apparently content simply to receive the multitude of honours that came his way, and from both sides of the divided Germany.

It is during this final period, in which he came to be recognized as a world literary figure, that, paradoxically, a more humorous and playfully erotic quality began to emerge in his writing. Works such as *The Holy Sinner* (1951), *The Black Swan* (1953) and, above all, *The Confessions of Felix Krull, Confidence Man* (1954) represent a new direction in Mann's work. Their subject matter is transgression, of the bounds of bourgeois respectability, of the boundaries between sin and sanctification, of the sexual proprieties of age and status. For that reason, some critics have found them embarrassingly difficult to integrate into the 'serious' Mannian corpus; but that embarrassment should be a cause for celebration. *Krull*, in particular, which tells of the exploits of a young hero intent on achieving success through native wit and charm of personality, deals with a number of highly contemporary themes: the power of game, the nature of identity and play acting, the androgynous nature of eroticism and the fallibility of descriptive language. It gave Mann particular pleasure to observe that he was able to resume work on the Krull novel on exactly the same page that he had left it in 1910. The first part of the novel was published in 1954; the second part was never completed. Thomas Mann died, quite suddenly, of a thrombosis the following year at his home in Switzerland, at the age of 80.

At the end of *Death in Venice*, Gustav von Aschenbach, the poet and aesthetic theorist, takes leave of his life under the most abject circumstances: slumped in his deck chair and donned in garish clothing and make-up, he has become the victim of his own illusion that the artist can stay clear of 'the abyss' of human knowledge without himself suffering as a consequence. It is, however, only the reader who is able to register the grim irony of Aschenbach's demise, for the mask of authorial respectability that he so carefully constructed throughout his career has remained fully intact in the eyes of an adoring public, which now takes shocked cognizance of the death of the great artist. Mann himself was only too aware of the dangers that existed for the artist in playing the role of a cultural *praeceptor* and, in his letters and diaries, gave full testimony to his many personal, political and intellectual shortcomings precisely to obviate the impression of authorial superiority that Aschenbach consciously cultivates. Notwithstanding such efforts, Mann came, nevertheless, in the final years of his life, to be celebrated as an elder statesman amongst modern writers, as one who would rank as a literary giant, even in the company of such writers as Hauptmann, Rilke and Kafka.[17]

It was inevitable that a reaction against Mann's reputation as the patrician of modern German literature would eventually set in. In the intellectual and cultural breadth of his work, Mann had made few concessions to his readership: he had always assumed that he was writing for a public that shared his own cultural heritage. As the post-war period drew on, such an assumption came increasingly to be regarded as elitist and politically unacceptable by a younger generation of readers and scholars who, excited by the more politically engaged writing of contemporaries such as Günter Grass and Heinrich Böll, began to find Mann's patrician demeanour at best irrelevant, at worst offensive. Hans Erich Nossack spoke for many when, in response to a questionnaire aimed at assessing Mann's popularity amongst contemporary writers, he dismissed the much lionized author as a 'lofty but slick poseur'.[18]

It is only by dint of much serious scholarship done in Germany and elsewhere, that Mann's reputation has been able to recover since its nadir in the 1960s and 1970s. The various contradictory aspects of Mann's writing are now being recognized as essential features of a highly complex literary personality, which thrived upon precisely the contradictions and volte-faces that his detractors have found so damaging. The latest research on Mann has allowed us to recognize that if his work is 'problematical', it is so in the best sense of the word, in the sense that makes the reading of his literature more, not less, stimulating.

# 2

# Decadence and the Decline of the Family: *Buddenbrooks*

Thomas Mann's first novel *Buddenbrooks* has remained his most popular; its publication in 1901 secured the basis for a literary reputation that was eventually to place Mann amongst the major novelists of modern European literature. One reason for the success of the novel lies in the fact that it can be read and enjoyed on a number of levels. At its simplest, it can be approached as a saga of the decline of a family, a process that is sensitively described in terms of the personal and domestic crises that befall that family over a period of almost half a century; on another level, it can be seen as a novel that bears witness to the crisis of an entire social class, the conservative burgher (*Bürger*) class, which, unable to come to terms with the accelerating historical changes that characterized the mid to late nineteenth century, eventually finds itself replaced by a more ruthless and pragmatic class of entrepreneurs; and, finally, the novel can be viewed as an exploration of a number of moral and philosophical themes, such as the desire for self-fulfilment versus duty to society, self-expression versus restraint, appearance versus reality and the fateful affinities between art and death. *Buddenbrooks* can also be seen as Mann's most autobiographical novel; not only are there obvious parallels between the Christian names of the central male members of the family and Mann's own, but the type of business they are engaged in (the buying and selling of wheat), and even the town they live in are drawn from the social background and personal circumstances of Mann's own life. The autobiographical dimension of the novel is, however, most evident in the very subject matter of the novel, which, in telling of an old established merchant family that comes to grief because

17

the sole remaining male heir grows to prefer the other-worldly consolations of music to the realities of the business world, directly parallels the predicament experienced by the young Thomas Mann whose early artistic leanings led him into a critical revaluation of the cultural heritage of the *Bürger* class from which he had come.

*Buddenbrooks* may have been Mann's most autobiographical novel, but it was also among his most epic. Any confessional tendency that might have arisen as a result of the personal origins of the narrative is displaced by the larger concern that the reader should recognize that the fate of the Buddenbrook family was also that of the social class to which they belonged, the educated middle-class, which was undergoing a crisis of moral and political identity during the period covered by the novel, 1835 to 1875. This was the period in which Germany experienced a social and economic upheaval that was, in a comparatively short time span, to transform it from a back-ward-looking semi-feudal society into one of the great dynamic world powers of the modern period. All this was generated by the hard-headed 'blood and iron' philosophy espoused by the new chancellor, Otto von Bismarck, who introduced a new spirit of realism and determination into the political and economic affairs of the nation. Under Bismarck, the political romantics who had preceded him were forced to give way to the pressures of *Realpolitik*: ideals to pragmatism, regionalism to national unity and the individual to the state. These were policies which, no doubt, met the needs of the hour; but much was lost in their implementation. Writing over a decade later, Mann listed (with more than a touch of his characteristic irony) the 'achievements' of this *Realpolitik*: 'the tempering and hardening of Germany into a "*Reich*", the entry of science into industry and industry into science, the regulation, cooling and turning to hostility of the patriarchal-human relationships of employer and worker [. . .]; emancipation and exploitation; power, power, power!'[19]

Such a rapid process of historical change had enormous repercussions, above all, for that section of society from which Mann himself had come: the traditional *Bürger* class. It was this class who had traditionally cultivated the things of the mind and the more idealistic values that had been associated with culture, philosophy and personal development; a constellation of values summed up in the concept *Bildung*. These were precisely the values that the new Germany (according to Mann) was coming to despise. Superannuated and deprived of its traditional cultural goals and self-image, the *Bürger* class was being forced to undergo a transformation that would culminate in its 'dehumanization and loss of soul, [its] *hardening* into the capitalistic-imperialistic bourgeois'.[20]

Mann chooses to concentrate upon the fate of a single family as a way of assessing the human consequences of these historical changes. It is an understandable focus. As Ernest Bramsted has shown in his seminal study of the ideology of the *Bürgertum* in the nineteenth century, the family was regarded by many as the 'organic cell of the nation, as a living emotional unity', which alone could fill the moral vacuum left by the decline of traditional religion and the influence of the Church after the French Revolution.[21] The family represented the moral community in practice; it was the form of social life that guaranteed the continuing existence of certain types of values and a certain type of culture. It is for this reason that *Buddenbrooks* is offered explicitly (in the sub-title of the novel) as the story of the decline of a *family*, and it is for the same reason that Mann devotes so much space to the internal development of the Buddenbrook family, structuring his narrative around a chronicle of personal events within the family: births, marriages and deaths, family ceremonies, scandals and professional opportunities. These are described in such detail that it is possible to reconstruct an exact chronology for them. As we shall see, when Mann comes to offer reasons for the decline of the family, he both looks outwards towards the broader changes taking place in the economy of a changing Germany, and inwards to the psychological and even biological formation of his characters. This highly successful combination of the objective and the subjective is one of the keys to the novel's success. But the medium through which these two realms meet is the family, and to explain the decline of the Buddenbrooks is not only to describe the individual members who are a part and cause of that decline, but also their attitude to the concept of the family itself. That concept changes with each successive male head of the family.

The novel opens in 1835 with Johann Buddenbrook the Elder, as head of the family and firm, celebrating the occupancy of the new home in Meng Straße. This is a portrait of the Buddenbrooks as an extended family, as an organic body that comprises all ages, from the eight year-old Tony through to Johann's ageing wife, Madame Antoinette Buddenbrook. The house-warming itself is an event of enormous symbolic import, and Mann builds around this occasion an almost mythical air of harmony, stability and benevolence. The nostalgic longing that Mann brings to his description of this world of innocence and security before the 'Fall' is almost tangible in the detail with which it is lovingly described. In this world, the father is a benevolent patriarch, presiding in his snow-white powdered hair and frilly garb, like a benevolent god over his abundant family, confident in a social order that is founded on 'mutual respect and deference'.[22]

That the novel should open in 1835 is also of significance, for the cultural values that are being celebrated here belong to that period of German culture that existed between 1815 and 1848 known as *Biedermeier*. This was a period in German history that enjoyed a culture that has been described as 'sober, modest, unpretentious, and yet [with] a prepossessing elegance'.[23] These values are fully evident in the Buddenbrook family and its household, which succeeds in combining a sense for the ornately classical (as evident in their style of clothing and furnishings) with a simple and down-to-earth appreciation of life (exempli-fied by the bonhomie and healthy appetites which accompany the house-warming). Even the realm of art is fully integrated into this ordered scheme of things. The lullabies hummed by Johann the Elder over his grand-daughter's cot and the eulogies penned by Jean Jacques Hoffstede, the town poet, stand, in their affectionate celebration of the simple pleasures of life, in sharp contrast to the asocial and exotic musical flights of fancy that the sickly Hanno Buddenbrook, Johann's great grandson, and the last male member of the family, will later turn to as a balm for his lonely and otherworldly sensibility. At this early stage in the family's development, art and music support rather than mock the notion of family life.

The institution of the family constitutes not only the social and moral heart of the Buddenbrook household; it is also the centre around which the firm of 'Johann Buddenbrook, Grain Merchants (founded 1786)' revolves. This investment of the personal in the commercial was at the heart of the Protestant ethos ascribed to by the German burgher classes, whose rise in the seventeenth and eighteenth centuries was largely due to an ability to reconcile financial gain and industry with a sense of religious purpose. The Buddenbrooks retain this combination of values as a guiding principle in their financial transactions; they are hard-headed business people, but temper their quest for profit by a sense of what is fair and just. Efficient in their business dealings and confident in their moral probity, the Buddenbrook family share the confidence that is inscribed above the very entrance to their home: 'Dominus providebit' ('God Will Provide').

With the transference of the firm to his son, who is also named Johann, a different set of values comes into play. The Consul shares his father's reverence for tradition and history; but what was, for Johann the Elder, an almost unconsciously held set of values and outlook on life, comes to be espoused by his son as a dogmatic article of faith. The difference in temperament between the two successive heads of the family is obvious in their contrasting attitudes to the demands made by Johann's eldest son, Gotthold, on the family's estate. For Johann the Elder, the issue is quite simple: Gotthold, by entering into an injudicious marriage, has disqualified himself from further claims upon the family; he should be treated with due consideration for his pecuniary needs, and then left to his own devices. For the Consul Buddenbrook, Gotthold's case gives rise to an intense period of moral, legal and financial scrutiny. In the end, father and son do arrive at the same decision; the former through sound instinct, the latter only after an elaborate process of calculation and moral self-scrutiny.

The younger Johann's attitude to the problem posed by Gotthold is typical of his concept of the family: it is a source of moral duty. Under his guidance (after the death of his father), the family gains 'weight' in the eyes of the community; but this increase in status is achieved at great cost. The Consul Buddenbrook elevates the notion of the family to such an exalted position that the feelings and wishes of its individual members come to be neglected. This is most obviously so in the case of the Consul's daughter, Tony Buddenbrook. Tony plays a secondary role in the conduct of the affairs of the family; but she is not without intellect or personality. Like many female characters in the novels of the nineteenth century (from Emma Bovary in Flaubert's *Madame Bovary* to Anna Karenina in Tolstoy's novel of the same name), her own personal development and preferences (which surface in her brief vacation 'romance' with the young Tom Schwarzkopf) are frustrated by the unsympathetic patriarchal morality into which she is born. The Consul's insistence that Tony should, in spite of her personal disinclination to do so, marry the highly unattractive Grünlich because the marriage will be 'highly advantageous for the family and the firm' shows how far we have come from the original picture of familial content with which the novel opened.[24] What Tony is encouraged to accept is satisfaction rather than happiness, and a feeling of self-importance arising out of her improved status within the family. It is one of the many ironies of the novel that Tony Buddenbrook is so amenable to her fate because she is 'saturated with her family history'.[25]

What the fate of Tony demonstrates is that the notion of family and firm has reified into a potentially dehumanizing and impersonal abstraction. This tendency is reinforced with the ascendancy of Thomas Buddenbrook, the Consul's son, to the head of the firm. The latter espouses a belief in family and firm, but cannot support such attestations with any real conviction. He can only exercise this position as a role, maintaining the appearance of commitment solely through an enormous act of willpower, whose influence he elaborates into a virtual philosophy. Like Gustav von Aschenbach in Mann's later novella, *Death in Venice*, Thomas Buddenbrook devotes the greatest part of his energies to hiding from the world his growing exhaustion. Although he frequently castigates Christian for the latter's lack of responsibility, Thomas shares many of his brother's exotic predilections, as shown by his choice of wife, the beautiful and musically gifted but over-refined, Gerda. Under his guidance, the family splinters into a collection of isolated individuals each going their separate ways: Thomas further and further into an absorption with the self and its anxieties; Gerda towards self-fulfilment in her illicit relationship with an officer; and Hanno towards the mystical delights of romantic music. Thomas is the patriarchal head who most clearly represents the transition between the burgher past of the family and its non-burgher future, a process that culminates in the figure of Thomas's one and only child, Hanno.

Hanno marks the end of the family both as a reality (he is the last living male member), and as a concept. Not only does the family cease to exist with him; he has absolutely no sense of the importance of the family as an institution, indeed, is 'a little contemptuous and supremely indifferent' to its very concept, as he dramatically demonstrates by violently crossing through the final page in the family almanac, a gesture which gains much of its powerful symbolism from the fact that Tony Buddenbrook had earlier inscribed her own name in the same volume precisely to symbolize the willing sacrifice of her individuality for the sake of the family.[26] Hanno reaches the point of complete alienation from the family, an attitude already intimated in the figures of Gotthold and Christian before him. In Hanno, biological and psychological decadence combine to make the continuation of the family morally undesirable and physically impossible. With his death, the story ends, the family extant now only in its remaining female members, who have come together to try and find in one another's company consolation for, and an explanation of, the hard lot that fate has dealt to the Buddenbrooks.

The Buddenbrooks' decline is, then, made manifest through the growing alienation that successive male heads of the family experience from the patrician burgher values held by their ancestors. But the question still remains about why these individuals should hold increasingly negative attitudes towards the family. To explain that, we must move our attention from the process of *decline* on to the notion of *decadence* that underwrites Mann's pessimistic account of this family. Here Mann works on a number of levels: socio-economic, biological and philosophical.

We can begin to unravel Mann's complex notion of decadence by making the obvious observation that, whilst *Buddenbrooks* is a story of the 'decline of a family', not all families in the novel are subject to such a fateful process. There is one family, in particular, who, practising a similar profession and enjoying a similar social standing, seems to flourish in the face of similar social and economic changes. Their success gives us a clue to the reasons for the decline of the Buddenbrook family. The Hagenströms make an early appearance in the novel, and from the very start a system of opposition is established between their 'zeal and ambition', and disregard for convention, and the 'rigid traditions of the older families', amongst whom are reckoned the Buddenbrooks.[27] The Hagenströms, 'free from the fetters of tradition and ancestral piety', represent the new entrepreneurial spirit that is the order of the day; they have not only adapted to change, but have understood how to exploit it to their own advantage. In contrast, the successive heads of the Buddenbrook family seem inept and anachronistic in their business dealings. They may not all share the views of Johann the Elder, who bemoans the growing professionalism of a world 'which thinks of nothing but mines and factories and making money', but the succeeding members of the family do retain the conviction that the Buddenbrook business can continue to be conducted simply as a *family* concern. This was a period which required an aggressive and risk-taking attitude to capital investment, and Johann's advice to his son: 'Attend with zeal to thy business by day, but do none that hinders thee from thy sleep at night' is clearly not in keeping with the dynamic entrepreneurial nature of the times.[28] The cynicism of the new financial world is represented by the usurer Kesselmeyer, who recites his credo to the nearly bankrupt Grünlich: 'one only keeps a thing as long as it is rising or at least keeping steady. When it begins to fall one sells'.[29] In contrast, capital for the Consul Buddenbrook is his total assets (including the family house) and his reputation, which he believes will continue alone to guarantee prosperity. Compared to the cut and thrust capitalism of the Hagenströms and types such as Kesselmeyer, Consul Buddenbrook's belief that 'faithful work always finds its reward' must strike the reader as at best naive, at worst economically catastrophic.[30]

A more aggressive attitude makes itself felt when Thomas takes over the firm after the death of his father; now the talk is of 'risks' and the utilization of credit, but, ominously, also of a 'daily struggle for success', carried on with an effort of 'will', and with a nostalgic glance back to a by-gone era when 'people were better off'.[31] Even at the very moment at which the Buddenbrook fortunes seem at their highest in the hands of the young heir, Mann foreshadows a time when Thomas will lose trade because he is 'too cautious and conscientious'.[32] The debate between himself and his sister Tony over whether to take a risk on the Pöppenrade harvest sums up Thomas's innate conservatism and lack of understanding of the changed economic climate. For him such transactions are made only by 'Jews' and 'cut throats', and not by firms who have their 'own traditions'. He adds: 'We have been in business a hundred years without touching that sort of transaction, and I have no idea of beginning at this late day'.[33] Failure to recognize a propitious economic prospect is not, however, the source of Thomas's decadence. It is not that he fails to act with regard to the Pöppenrade harvest; he does act, but for the wrong reasons. Once Tony has left the scene of the debate, Thomas's principled position collapses, and, in a fit of belated self-affirmation, he resolves, without further consideration, to go through with the transaction. This act of assertion, founded on such a hollow base, fails, and in doing so spells the beginning of the end for the family's fortunes.

The Hagenström family not only exceeds the Buddenbrooks in terms of financial kudos and material success; it also proves to be more prolific in its fertility. At the same time as the Hagenström clan is increasing, the Buddenbrook family is contracting, until it reaches the point where Hanno is the single remaining male heir, and its issue ceases entirely. This lack of fecundity is associated with the second cause for the family's decline: its biological and genetic decadence. The physical decadence of the Buddenbrook family is evident from the very start of the novel, where we learn that the young Thomas Buddenbrook, who is at this time barely nine years, possesses teeth which are 'not very good, being small and yellowish'.[34] It only becomes clear later in the novel that the state of a character's teeth are an indicator of his more general health. Thus, the young Tom Schwarzkopf (whose youthful charm and sincerity win Tony's heart) has 'unusually regular teeth, glistening in close ranks of polished ivory', unlike the young Hanno Buddenbrook whose teeth are 'particularly bad', and require frequent treatment. These almost incidental equations of poor teeth and decadence culminate in the death of Thomas Buddenbrook, who collapses and dies after receiving treatment for a tooth that is 'decayed' ('hohl').[35] A similar process of equating physical attributes with psychological and even moral characteristics takes place in the many references to hands and eyes and, more obviously, in the numerous references to appetite and eating, all of which are developed into an important network of *leit-motifs* in the novel.

These symptoms of physical decay are signs of a more thorough biological decline, which becomes more manifest with each successive male head of the Buddenbrook family. The nature of this form of decadence is also sounded in the early pages of the novel during the height of the house-warming festivities. In a characteristic way, Mann, after having set up a scene of family contentment and harmony, and in the midst of general merriment and gaiety, undermines the domestic idyll by introducing the case of the wayward Gotthold, whose attempts to exert emotional blackmail on the family and firm point to a residual lack of moral probity that will only fully emerge later in the figure of Christian Buddenbrook. Far more ominous, however, than the objective threat of Gotthold's demands on the family is Consul Buddenbrook's response to them. As the celebration party begins to move towards the dining-room, the Consul Buddenbrook, in a gesture that will become character-istic of him, reaches for a document in his inside pocket, containing news of an incipient family scandal. The narrator then adds the telling note: 'The polite smile had left his face, giving place to a strained and care-worn look, and the muscles stood out on his temples as he clenched his teeth. For appearance's sake, he made a few steps towards the dining room . . .'.[36] It is a brief passage, but one that foreshadows the strain, nervous energy and incipient exhaustion that will fully emerge in the behaviour of his son, Thomas. In him, the last male head of the Buddenbrook family, the process of biological decadence reaches a critical stage. Unable physically to cope with the growing number of financial crises that beset the firm, Thomas is forced to invest increasingly greater amounts of energy in an effort 'to conceal his inner decline', to ensure that his essential lack of energy and vitality remains hidden from friends and foe alike.[37] Talk is now of the 'mask' that is donned in a daily ritual, to 'preserve the dehors', as the financial fortunes of the family inexorably dwindle. When the mask does eventually drop, and Thomas comes to fully confront his own nihilism and aboulia, it seems a logical consequence of his position that he will look for the solution to his predicament, not in an improvement of self, but in its extinction.

He is helped along this path by a chance encounter with the writings of the German philosopher, Arthur Schopenhauer, who, with Friedrich Nietzsche and Richard Wagner, was one of the great influences on the young Thomas Mann. In one of his recurring states of dejection, Thomas quite by chance looks into Schopenhauer's *magnum opus*, *The World as Will and Representation* (first published in 1818). As he reads, he finds his view on life transformed. What Thomas learns from Schopenhauer is that the individualistic philosophy that had underwritten the important historical changes of the nineteenth century, changes which the Hagenströms and others had so keenly grasped, are all fictions. Ambition, the striving for success, self-realization, the assertion of will upon the world, even the desire for off-spring and the continuation of family name and tradition, can be forgotten because they are all emanations of an incessant life force, a blind, thoughtless 'urging will' that will never rest, and of which we are all a part, a fact that makes individual striving as pointless as it is futile. When we die, we do not disappear; we simply merge back into an all-embracing and impersonal life force.[38]

Thomas' longing for the extinction of self reaches its apogee in the short life of his son, Hanno. With Hanno the mask has finally dropped; there is now no longer any effort expended in dissimulation; the burden of weakness that is at the core of the Buddenbrook constitution is finally allowed to emerge and manifest itself for what it truly is: a longing for death. Hanno gives vent to this longing on a number of occasions;[39] but it is through Hanno's deep sympathy with music that it finds its most eloquent and persuasive expression. Although music was the quintessential German art form, the medium through which the German character had, particularly during the nineteenth century, best been able to express itself, Mann was aware of the dangers which resided in its purity and emotional appeal. Particularly in the work of the late Romantic Richard Wagner, it had the power to bring those held in its sway by its magic to a point of near mystical intoxication. This is exactly how Hanno responds to music. In his eyes, it is far more than the simple source of entertainment that it had been for Buddenbrook the Elder at the commencement of the novel; for the sickly and introspective Hanno, bereft of human contact, it is a means of transcendence, a way out of the social sphere with its onerous duties and moral obligations, and into a world of pure interiority. The affinity between this world and death is, however, unmistakeable, as is made clear in the very last piece of music Hanno plays: Beethoven's piano sonata, Opus 24. Hanno's treatment of the closing bars perfectly expresses his desire to be gone from life entirely: 'Then, at last, at last; in the weariness after excess, a long, soft *arpeggio* in the minor trickled through, mounted a tone, resolved itself in the major, and died in mournful lingering away' ('mit einem wehmütigen Zögern erstarb').[40]

Thomas Buddenbrook's own glimpse of Nirvana lasts but a

single day. As a new day dawns, he forgets his Schopenhauerian inspiration, and turns to seek solace in the more familiar world of Christian teaching, before dying (in an act of typically Mannian bathos) of a heart attack induced by a visit to the dentist. Thomas' immersion in the writings of Schopenhauer turns out to be a temporary and dubious flight into philosophy, so that he can receive 'justification and licence for his sufferings', and legitimate what is clearly a growing death-wish. The Schopenhauer episode also raises one final question about whether, along with its socio-economic and biological manifestations, the decadence that afflicts the male members of the Buddenbrook family is the consequence of a specific philosophy of life. There seems good reason to believe that it is, for long before Thomas discovers the consolation of Schopenhauer's philosophy he gives voice to a highly pessimistic worldview that sees life as a constant struggle between competing forces for power and success. In such a scheme of things, only those who are supremely fit, who enjoy 'the one raw, naked, dominating instinct of self-preservation' will survive; the others will, sooner or later, go under.[41] And Thomas Buddenbrook, with his introverted and self-questioning temperament and his increasing predilection for surface finery, knows that he does not belong to the new breed of men who have come to prominence in the commercial world, those 'practical men, more naturally, more vigorously, more impeccably practical than he was himself'. It is a view of the world that owes much to the theory of natural selection proposed by Charles Darwin. The latter, it is true, is never mentioned by name, but the sense of struggle that Thomas intuits beneath the surface of his contemporary business world and the fatalism with which he interprets the declining fortunes of the family fully accord with the philosophy of one of Germany's foremost proponents of Darwinian theory: Ernst Haeckel. The latter's bleak view on existence might well have provided a motto for the fate of the Buddenbrook family: 'Only through progressive movement are life and development possible. Standing still is in itself regression, and regression carries with it death'.[42]

Mann offers, then, a complex cluster of explanations for the decline of the Buddenbrook family, but leaves it to the reader to bring this configuration into alignment and make the final decision about the reasons for that decline. In this task, the reader can expect little help from the omniscient narrator, who not only refuses to offer ultimate explanations for the behaviour of the characters, but also refuses to pass judgement on them. Instead, the narrative voice retains an epic distance from the events it relates, eschewing emotional evocation and moral commentary in favour of a point of view that is (as Mann himself noted) 'quite without pathos, rhetoric and sentimentality, but, rather, of a pessimistic, humorous and fatalistic inclination'.[43]

Mann's ability to register the personal predicament of his characters at a distance (and even with some humour), whilst withholding judgement upon them is the source of his often noted ironic perspective. The narrator encourages the reader to hold in equilibrium a variety of contrary emotions towards the characters, to sympathize with them whilst rejecting their positions, to regret their fates whilst seeing them as objectively necessary. Since the events and characters described in *Buddenbrooks* were largely drawn from Mann's own private life, it is understandable that he should wish to retain a distance from them. Thomas Buddenbrook, in particular, Mann tells us, was a figure for whom he sympathized a great deal, calling him 'the mystical-threefold image of father, offspring and double'.[44] But Mann's distanced point of view was also the result of his intention to see the fate of his family as part of an epochal change in the social structure of Europe, and this required an epic scope capable of registering both the *subjective* and human tragedy of the Buddenbrook family, whilst, at the same time, seeing it as part of an *objective* train of events set in motion by important historical changes. Mann was helped in his task by the example of writers such as the Norwegian novelists Alexander Kielland and Jonas Lie, whose own portrayals of the rise and fall of noted families had become something of a genre by the time Mann began work on his own novel.

What Thomas Mann has in common with such writers, and with others such as Balzac and Tolstoy, is a concern to provide a balance between subjective experience and objective context. *Buddenbrooks* comes towards the end of the great period of Realist literature, which began with the work of Dickens and Balzac in the 1830s and 1840s and terminated half a century later in the work of writers such as Emile Zola and the brothers Goncourt, in whose hands it developed into a movement called 'Naturalism'. Aspects of these literary movements are evident in

Mann's novel; the humanistic breadth, the balance between humour and tragedy and the detail and monumentality of Realism are complemented by a concern with the processes of social and biological decay and an interest in psychology that had its sources in Naturalism. Even the style of Naturalist writing, which often aimed at a scientific depiction of events, is evident in Mann's novel (notably in the description of the death of Hanno).[45] Mann does not employ these various literary techniques for their own sake; they are used because they are apt to the event or character under description. When he wishes to communicate the monumentality and solidity of the Buddenbrook world, for example, he employs a typically Realist epic point of view, which strives after a detailed recording of externals as, for example, in the detail lavished on the victuals consumed by the family during the house-warming.[46] On other occasions, when it is necessary to impart a sense of the psychology of the protagonists (such as the embarrassment of young Hanno expected to recite in front of his parental audience), the narrator adopts a device known as 'free indirect style' (called in German 'erlebte Rede') which allows him, by taking on their language and point of view, to capture the innermost feelings of his characters.[47]

*Buddenbrooks* may look to the past; but it also looks to the future. Its most immediate context is not that of Realism or even Naturalism, but that combination of aesthetic, literary and philosophical impulses that appeared towards the end of the nineteenth century, and which we call 'Modernism'. The great modernist writers of this period, such as James Joyce, Virginia Woolf, Marcel Proust and Franz Kafka, attempted to break away from what they saw to be the purely mimetic or descriptive nature of earlier fiction, preferring the symbolic nature of experience. In their fiction, objects are often depicted not for their own sake, but because they give the reader a glimpse into a deeper reality. A similar technique is used in *Buddenbrooks*, and is evident even in those passages that appear purely circumstantial. Something similar to the following description of the furnishings of the Buddenbrook family home, for example, might be found in any Realist novel of the nineteenth century: 'The room was hung with heavy resilient tapestries put up in such a way that they stood well out from the walls. They were woven in soft tones to harmonize with the carpet, and they depicted idyllic landscapes in the style of the eighteenth century, with merry vinedressers, busy husbandmen, and gaily beribboned shepherdesses who sat beside crystal streams with spotless lambs in their laps or exchanged kisses with amorous shepherds. These scenes were usually lighted by a pale yellow sunset to match the yellow coverings on the white enamelled furniture and the yellow silk curtains at the two windows'.[48]

This passage (like so many in Mann's novel) works on a number of levels. In one sense, it simply sets the scene and gives shape and substance to the physical environment of the Buddenbrook family, denoting comfort and a refined life style; but on another level, this environment (particularly the tapestry) can be read as a symbolic statement about the family and their outlook on life. The tapestry (which is, significantly, eighteenth rather than nineteenth century in origin) depicts a world of harmony and plenty, of innocence and productivity, of the rural rather than the urban: values that are a part of the self-image of the Buddenbrook family at this stage in its development. But even in this world of unblemished innocence and self-confidence, the narrator cannot resist the qualifying comment that what we are seeing here (and, by extension, in the world of the family itself) is an idyll, something not of the world, an unreality. It is a brief circumstantial passage, but one that anticipates the major theme of the novel: the tendency of the Buddenbrook family to live in the past and to avoid confrontation with the present.

Mann was to build this concern for the symbolic import of realist detail into his most noted literary technique: the *leit-motif*. In its original music form, the *leit-motif* was a note or sound cluster that, once associated with a character or theme, came to invoke the latter in different situations. In the literary technique of Thomas Mann, the *leit-motif* came to be used to refer to those subjects, gestures or phrases which, through their regular appearance in the course of the story, aquire symbolic import. *Leit-motifs* appear in *Buddenbrooks* in a number of ways: as physical characteristics (such as poor teeth), as gestures (such as Thomas' nervous twitch) or as idiosyncrasies of speech; and as natural or man-made objects that possess symbolic weight. The Buddenbrook family home belongs in this latter category. Both its deteriorating physical condition and its changing ownership, which passes from the Buddenbrooks to Hagenströms, tell us much about the decline of the family. The sea is also in this category; it does not change, but the responses to it made by individual members of the family do. Through the course of the novel, various members of the Buddenbrook family travel to the sea at Travenmünde; as a young girl, Tony Buddenbrook visits it, as does her nephew, Hanno, a number of years later. The goal of the two visits is the same: relaxation and recovery from stress at home, but there the similarity ends. For what is for Tony a source of invigoration and inspiration and a portent of 'freedom' becomes for the world-weary Hanno a means of escaping the world, a medium through which the self is lost in a 'green and blue infinity beyond', making it possible to 'submerge all consciousness of time and space'.[49] Far from connoting freedom, the sea for Hanno is an early symbol of his wish to be gone from the world, to die.

Apart from its style, the modernism of *Buddenbrooks* is also evident in its philosophical attitude to the world. We discussed irony earlier as point of view, as if it were simply a narrative technique allowing Mann to depict the personal plight of his characters without sentiment or excessive value judgement. But the ironic perspective presupposes a series of values: a preference for knowledge rather than simple experience, for complexity rather than simplicity, for psychology rather than action, in short, for art rather than life. It is a set of values that belongs to the literary culture of *fin de siècle* Europe, and particularly to the intellectual influence of one of its most original philosophers: Friedrich Nietzsche. Nietzsche was one of the great cultural critics of his age, castigating, in a series of works published between 1870 and 1900 (such as *Untimely Meditations* (1876) and *The Twilight of the Idols* (1889)), the German (and European) bourgeoisie for their vulgarity, commercialism and utilitarianism. When the narrator deplores changes in the school system that have caused 'joyous idealism' to be replaced with the new idols of 'authority, duty, power, service, the career', he is taking from Nietzsche the latter's rejection of the nationalistic pomposity and inflated self-esteem that characterized his contemporary Germany after its successful war against France and its unification in 1871.[50] Because in such a world 'health' and 'normalcy' are equated with a rampant anti-intellectualism and savage disregard for art, and in a society that is systematically excluding human values from the public realm, the sensitive individual is forced to give up on the external world and turn inward towards introspection and the purely aesthetic. The result is 'decadence', a fateful combination of knowledge, sickness and social alienation, which Mann inscribes into the figures of Thomas and, particularly, Hanno Buddenbrook.

Mann does not himself, however, although an artist, give a personal credence to this constellation of values. And here we come to the second Nietzschean concept that influencd Mann: that of 'self-overcoming' ('Selbstüberwindung'). For, in one important sense, the Buddenbrooks story does not end with the death of Hanno in 1877, but with the writing and publication of that story as a novel in 1901. In the final analysis, the novel might best be understood not as an historical novel (in any sense of that term), but as an autobiography imposed upon history. Mann's sympathies with decadence (which he shared with a generation of writers) are prevented from becoming destructive by being sublimated into their study: the novel, *Buddenbrooks*. It is in this final act, in which the autobiographical becomes literary artifice, that a new definition of the artistic vocation becomes evident: the text as vanquished life. It is this strategy of composition, in which the pathos of experience is overcome by a distance made possible through irony and historical relativization, that takes Thomas Mann into Modernism proper, and into the great mature works of *Death in Venice*, *The Magic Mountain* and *Doctor Faustus* that were to follow his first novel.

# 3

# The Artist and Society: *Tristan, Tonio Kröger* and the Early Stories

---

*Buddenbrooks* can be regarded as the pinnacle of Thomas Mann's early fiction. Between its completion in 1901 and the publication of his second major novel, *The Magic Mountain* in 1924, lay a period of almost a quarter of a century. During that time, Mann finished a further novel, *Royal Highness* (1909) and published a series of short stories and novella, notably *Tristan* (1903), *Tonio Kröger* (1903) and *Death in Venice* (1912). *Royal Highness* is a deceptively light-hearted novel; underneath its idyllic story line of a provincial German prince falling in love with a gifted and highly self-conscious American girl lies a more serious (albeit entirely affectionate) study of the clash between the anachronistic mores of traditional Germany and the moneyed opportunism of the new world, between the competing forms of government of monarchy and democracy, and, indeed, between the overlaps and divisions between the private sphere of the family and the public sphere of politics. But this was a side to the novel not fully appreciated by his contemporaries, who expected the tragic undertones of his Buddenbrook study to be further explored. As Mann himself later admitted, the novel was a little too self-consciously on the side of life, too obviously the product of a writer satisfied with his lot and the social order.[51] It is Mann in his minor mode.

It is only in his short stories and novella that Mann once again takes up some of the major themes of *Buddenbrooks*: the relationship between sickness and knowledge, the insatiability of longing, self-fulfilment versus duty to society, the clash between aesthetic sensibility and morality, and the affinities between music and death. Mann had broached such themes as early as 1898, the year in which he published his first book of short stories, *Der kleine Herr Friedemann* (*Little Herr Friedemann*). The title story of that volume anticipates *Buddenbrooks* in a number of ways, notably in the parallels between its central character, the handicapped Johannes Friedemann, and the sickly Hanno Buddenbrook, who share not only a flawed physical constitution, but also a certain inflection of artistic sensibility. Like Hanno, Johannes lives on the margin of society, modestly sustaining himself on vicarious pleasures drawn from music and the theatre, remaining an observer of life rather than a participant. But there the similarities end, for little Herr Friedemann does not stay aloof from the world, but becomes passionately, and fatally, involved in it. This involvement begins with his first glimpse of the exotic Frau Rinnlingen, the allegedly wayward wife of the District Commandant, who acts as a catalyst upon Johannes, rousing in him 'all those forces which from his youth up he had sought to suppress'.[52] The equanimity of his previous stoical existence now gives way to a tortured longing for the love object. That this love is destined to remain unrequited soon becomes clear to him and, as the prescience of his inevitable failure increases, so does the trauma of his attenuated sensibility. He becomes the victim of his own love sickness, torn between an 'exalted state' one moment, and 'impotent rage' the next. The story 'Little Herr Friedemann' anticipates *Buddenbrooks* also in the resolution that both characters find to their sufferings. Like Hanno, Johannes also looks for a solution to his crisis of sensibility in an extinction of the self, as, following his final rejection by the beloved, he gives himself over to a watery grave; but unlike Hanno's gentle passage out of this world, little Herr Friedemann's final moment is dominated by a death-wish that is mingled with an anger and 'an insane rage', which he directs as much against himself as against a world that provides, in the form of distant laughter, a cruelly mocking valediction to his end.[53]

Little Herr Friedemann is marked off from society both through his physical deformity and through the intensity of the emotions with which he confronts experience. Early in the story he asks himself the question: 'Is not life in and for itself a good, regardless of whether we may call its content "happiness"?', and

answers with an affirmative that is ironically undermined by his
eventual fate.[54] Nevertheless, in his openness to experience, and
in his highly-tuned sensibility, he reaches, like Hanno Buddenbrook after him, a quality of judgement on the world that can
fairly be called 'artistic'. In this respect, he has much in common
with many of the characters who appear in Thomas Mann's
other short stories of the period, the great majority of which deal
with the problem of the artist in society, and, more particularly,
with the problem of the asocial nature of the artistic sensibility.
Mann's interest in the figure of the artist was shared by a
number of other major writers of the modernist period, such as
E. M. Forster, James Joyce and Marcel Proust. For these writers
and others, the artist was a symbol of those values of the creative
mind threatened by an increasingly materialist and technological
civilization. Such a world had little place for the non-material,
non-quantifiable aspects of experience, for imagination, phantasy and the sense of the ineffable mystery of things. It is these
qualities that the artist embodies, but in doing so condemns
himself to a position of alienation from the normal course of
society.

As his sensitive treatment of Hanno Buddenbrook in the novel
*Buddenbrooks* showed, Mann shared the concern of his contemporaries for the plight of the artist in the modern world. There is
simply no place in the highly functional bureaucratic society of
Wilhelminian Germany for Hanno's almost mystical feel for
music. And yet, as Mann's approach in his early stories indicates, the problem is a complex one. We cannot simply assume
that all artists are in touch with the divine afflatus, whilst all
*Bürger* are representatives of a banal and mindless materialism.
Indeed, does not true art depend to a large degree upon contact
with the society that it says it despises, and should we not also
make a distinction between true artists and those who simply
style themselves as such? Mann himself, in fact, was one who
stood astride both worlds, a position that allowed him to explore
the equation 'artist versus society' from a number of quite
different angles in the stories and novella he wrote between 1900
and 1914, a period which saw the publication of some of his most
successful and thought-provoking works, such as *Tonio Kröger*
and *Death in Venice*.

Many of the artist figures who appear in these early stories are
treated in a positive fashion, with respect and sympathy for their

plight; but others are presented as self-indulgent poseurs, restless creatures who prefer the image of 'the artist' to the hard work necessary to sustain the reality of the creative process. Little Herr Friedemann represents one type of artistic sensibility; although not a producing artist, the visceral intensity of his emotions (which allows the narrator to talk of his adoration of the loved one in terms of an 'attack' and a 'seizure') links him to characters such as Praisegod Piepsam (in 'The Way to the Churchyard' (1900)). Like Johannes Friedemann, Piepsam experiences the world in such an unreflectively intense way that he eventually falls victim to his own emotional torment. The latter's sense of alienation produces such an extreme sense of rage against society (and is sparked off by such a trivial incident) that the reader is encouraged to feel pity for, but not sympathy with, his excessive response. His strictures against a youth unlawfully riding a bicycle along a path to the village churchyard are treated with comic detachment by the narrator: 'Never was seen such a sight. A man raving mad on the way to the churchyard, a man with his face swollen with roaring, a man dancing with rage, capering, flinging his arms about, quite out of control. The bicycle was out of sight by this time, but still Piepsam stood where he was and raved'.[55]

The characters in Mann's other stories, such as Detlev in 'The Hungry' (1902) or the hero of 'The Dilettante' (1897), register their alienation with greater insight and judgement. Like almost all of these artist figures, the dilettante is 'shut out, unregarded, disqualified, unknown, *hors ligne – declassé*, pariah, a pitiable object' even to himself, but his response is not the rage or emotional reaction evinced by little Herr Friedemann or Piepsam, but a quiet resignation that gives opportunity for self-analysis. Like little Herr Friedemann, the dilettante is also the victim of unrequited love (in his case of the more accessible daughter of the local Q.C.). But this time there is a twist to the tale. For what prevents the dilettante from obtaining his loved one (who stands, in all of these stories, for acceptance into bourgeois society) is not only the familiar difficulty of winning the attention and favours of the other, but a more obscure obstacle that has its origins in the dilettante's own indecisiveness and lack of determination, not only to confront the girl when the opportunity arises but, and more importantly, to explore the real reasons for his pursuit of her. The dilettante is given to introspection, but it is an introspection which evades rather than confronts reality; until it is too late. Only after all has been lost (with the engagement of the daughter to another suitor) can the dilettante admit to the reader that: 'love was the mere pretext, escape, and hope of salvation for my feelings of envy, hatred and self-contempt'.[56]

The case of the dilettante reveals the dilemma of the artist: he wants to belong to the social world, but is unable (or unwilling) to surrender his highly personal sense of self and identity in order to do so. Viewed from this angle, the artistic sensibility contains a noble component; but it also possesses a negative side in its self-absorption and in a bad conscience which leads to a perverse enjoyment of the experience of alienation for its own sake. The real artist (Mann implies) might have created something out of such an impasse, but not the dilettante; he fully deserves his name by refusing to turn his experiences into literature, for, as he concludes: 'one does not die of an unhappy love-affair. One revels in it. It is not such a pad pose'.[57] The dilettante, in short, has no intention of abandoning the melodramatic potential inherent in his own crisis of identity. In the final analysis, the reader's pity for him is obviated by the dilettante's own tortuous and highly elaborate sense of self-pity.

The dilettante's reference to the enjoyment of pose (even of one that is the fruit of conflict and loss) brings us to yet another type of artist depicted in Mann's early short stories: the artist as poseur. This is the theme of 'The Infant Prodigy' (1903). In that short story, Mann provides an insight into the ambiguous nature of artistic performance: it is a genuine expression of self, the result of inner reservoirs of talent and inspiration expressed in moments of oblivion and solitude; but it is also something manufactured for public consumption, the product of artifice and commercial enterprise. The pianist prodigy, Bibi Saccellaphylaccas, embodies precisely this mixture of 'charlatanry and [. . .] sacred fire'.[58] As such, he is the first in a long line of artists in Mann's writings, from Gustav von Aschenbach through to Felix Krull, who live in a twilight world between personal artistic commitment and public persona. The moral of this story is that the artist needs to take from both worlds, and Mann, himself adept at public performances, would have concurred with the concluding sentiments of the story: 'We are all infant prodigies, we artists'.

The nature of the inauthentic artist is addressed even more directly in a later story, 'At the Prophet's' (1904). This is a gentle satire on the world of false artistry, a world that held its temptations for the young Mann, but which he successfully resisted. The autobiographical component is evident in an unmistakeable way in the description of the main character and narrator of the story, a 'novelist, a man with a stiff hat and trim moustache', who confesses that he is more at home amongst middle-class circles than amongst this coterie of self-styled artists. The society into which this alter ego of Mann stumbles is dominated by a view of art as an esoteric exercise, as the product of a sensibility tortured by its own excessive longing. This is the world of the artist as bohemian, where 'pale young geniuses, criminals of the dream, sit with folded arms and brood', and where 'solitary and rebellious artists, inwardly consumed, hungry and proud, wrestle in a fog of cigarette smoke with devastatingly ultimate ideals'.[59] The key phrases do not require the relativizing inverted commas for their ironic use to be apparent, for Mann leaves us in little doubt that the 'ultimate ideas' discussed by the 'geniuses' are the products of highly self-conscious posturing egos. In his description of this milieu, Mann captures that peculiar mixture of aestheticism and primitivism which characterized the 'decadent' culture of *fin de siècle* Europe from the work of Huysmans in France to Stefan George in Germany. These values come to the fore in the reading undertaken by the host of the party, the 'spiritual lord' who, well fortified by red wine, unleashes an hour long panegyric upon a subject unknown (and unknowable). As the disbelieving narrator wryly observes: 'The solitary ego sang, raved, commanded. It would lose itself in confused pictures, go down in an eddy of logical error, to bob up again suddenly and startingly in an entirely unexpected place. Blasphemies and hosannas – a waft of incense and a reek of blood. In thunderings and slaughterings the world was conquered and redeemed'. Intended to transport the listener to a higher plane, this discourse leaves Mann's sober alter ego more than a little unmoved: 'The novelist sought in vain for a comfortable position for his aching back. At ten o'clock he had a vision of a ham sandwich but manfully put it away'.[60]

Mann treats this world of bohemian artistry with a good deal of humour aimed at deflating its self-importance and dismantling the aura with which it surrounds literature. His satirical picture has, however, an entirely serious point; what this clique of self-proclaimed geniuses neglects are precisely those aspects of the human condition required for art and literature to be more than an aesthetic ritual: the human element, 'a little feeling, a little yearning, a little love'.[61] The task of infusing life into art is not, however, an easy one. This message forms the theme of the short story 'A Weary Hour' (1905). Like the 'heroes' of Mann's previous stories, the protagonist of 'A Weary Hour' (who is modeled on Schiller) is 'a fugitive, oppressed and hungry, at odds with the world'; but unlike these earlier heroes, he is not consumed by a feeling of self-degradation (as little Herr Friedemann is), nor does he become, like Praisegod Piepsam, the victim of an impotent rage or give himself over to a perverse enjoyment of the problems encountered in reconciling self with the world; on the contrary, his sense of distance from the world is the basis upon which he produces works of literature that embody and, at the same time, transcend the pain that is their source.

Mann's story takes the form of a soliloquy upon the dedication demanded of the artist if he is to create art out of the intractable material of life, and the reader is encouraged to have at least respect for the 'nobility of his suffering', as he seeks perfection from his admittedly meagre gifts. The theme of weariness sounded in its title is carried throughout the whole story until it is silenced by the completion of the hero's literary task. This is a portrait of the artist as the self-overcomer, for the hero of this story must learn to give up a certain human contact with the world for the sake of his artistic achievement. But what is the cost of such renunciation? The answer is not forthcoming in this short story, but the affinities between the hero of 'A Weary Hour' and the hero of Mann's later novella *Death in Venice*, Gustav von Aschenbach (the achievement of office and honours, the life lived on the edge of exhaustion and the heroic determination to continue in the face of the diminution of inspiration) suggest that this is a type of artistic sensibility that also needs to be approached with an admiration hedged by caution. Above all, it is the presence in the story of another artist (whom we are meant to recognize as Goethe, 'who had only to open his god-like lips and straightway call the bright unshadowed things he saw by name'), which serves to remind the reader that not all artists require an heroic exertion of will to create their art, that at least some are able to create art out of generosity rather than restraint, out of health rather than sickness.[62]

The idea that art occupies a place nearer sickness than health forms the main theme for the first of two longer studies of the conflict between artistic sensibility and the world: *Tristan* (1903). Aptly set in a sanatorium, the story tells how a terminally ill married woman from the bourgeois class establishes a relationship with a young artist through their common fascination with the music of Wagner. The plot had the potential for a romance, and would have presented Mann with the opportunity for making fully explicit the critique of bourgeois society that was only implicit in *Buddenbrooks*, since the delicacy and frailty of the woman is juxtaposed to the raw and even vulgar health of her businessman husband and their child. But Mann prevents the story from developing in this direction. The attraction is never consummated, and the conflict between the artist and the bourgeois is resolved in favour of the latter rather than the former.

In *Tristan*, Mann engages, once again, with the theme of the inauthentic artist first dealt with in 'At the Prophet's'. But if that latter story paints a milieu, *Tristan* paints a character: Detlev Spinell. Spinell combines the asocial, haughty demeanour embodied in the heroes of 'The Hungry' (1902) and 'Disillusionment' (1896) with that proclivity to self-stylization and pose that characterized 'The Dilettante' (1897) and 'The Infant Prodigy' (1903). Spinell also represents a caricature of the ascetic hero of 'A Weary Hour'. Like the latter, he sees himself as the victim of his own high artistic standards, which require 'decorum' and a strict 'hygienic regime'; in Spinell's case, however, these do not result in a noble struggle with an intractable artistic subject matter, but with the 'heroic' effort involved in getting up early and having a cold bath.

Spinell's self-aggrandizement and inflated self-esteem are, then, treated with a good deal of ironic humour. But it is in his effect upon the ailing Frau Klöterjahn, who has been deposited in the sanatorium by her husband on account of a nascent tubercular complaint, that Spinell's otherwise harmless affectations acquire a more morally reprehensible significance. To Spinell, convinced of the necessary relationship between sickness and art, and of 'the frightfully unhealthy, undermining, irritating' nature of 'our whole inner life', the consumptive and

ethereal Frau Klöterjahn is the embodiment of genuine artistic
sensibility. After a brief introduction, he proceeds to re-write her
personal life history and to imply a breach with her husband that
is only a figment of his wishful thinking. More serious is his
incitement to her to resume her interest in music and, contrary
to her doctor's orders, expend her modest stock of energy in
playing the piano. The piece he encourages her to play is the
third act of Wagner's opera *Tristan and Isolde*, a highly symbolic
choice since it culminates in the famous *Liebestod* (love-death)
duet between the two lover protagonists. For Spinell, the music
speaks in a highly romantic way of the mystical consummation
of love possible through the ecstasy of death. In an extended
piece of *erlebte Rede*, the narrator records the final moments of
the two lovers: 'Their voices rose in mystic unison, rapt in the
worldless hope of that death-in-love, of endless oneness in the
wonder-kingdom of the night. Sweet night! Eternal night of love!
And all-encompassing land of rapture!'.[63] But, the music
finished, death in its more banal fashion asserts itself and, in
spite of medical intervention, Frau Klöterjahn finally succumbs
to her illness.

Frau Klöterjahn's death brings about the confrontation between the 'artist' Spinell and her 'bourgeois' husband. Spinell's
letter to Herr Klöterjahn (in which he accuses the latter of
repressing the natural aesthetic bent of his wife) turns into an
exposition of his artistic credo. For Spinell art is associated with
'decadence, decay', a combination that finds its ideal objective
correlative in music, itself 'full of that melancholy understanding
which is ripeness for death'. Into this peaceful world (Spinell
argues) the wooing Klöterjahn intruded, and the concluding
remarks of Spinell's letter sum up the rage and anger felt by the
whole regime of affronted artists in Mann's early works: 'I hate
you and your child, as I hate the life of which you are the
representative: cheap, ridiculous, but yet triumphant life, the
everlasting antipodes and deadly enemy of beauty'.[64]

It is typical of the limitations of Spinell's way of dealing with
the world that he can only fashion his critique of Klöterjahn in
the form of a letter, and it is equally typical of Klöterjahn that he
responds in person. Inarticulate, repetitive, overly corporeal,
Klöterjahn is, nevertheless, able to highlight the romantic falsi-
fication of his wife's life perpetrated by Spinell; not music but
cookery, not poetry but recipes for potato cakes constituted the

actual interests of Frau Klöterjahn who, unlike Spinell, did not flee from reality but lived in the world of the here and now. The final blow to the reader's willingness to accept Spinell's credentials as an artist is not, however, provided by Klöterjahn, but by his off-spring. It is highly significant that, in a novella where death has been seen both as a form of romantic intoxication, and as a crude fact of nature, the final gesture in the story should be left to an emissary of replete, unthinking life, in the shape of Klöterjahn's child. Out walking one morning Spinell encounters father and son coming towards him on the same path, the latter in full cry: 'his mouth gaped open till all the rosy gums were displayed; and as he shouted he rolled his head about in excess of mirth. Herr Spinell turned round and went thence. Pursued by the youthful Klöterjahn's joyous screams he went away across the gravel, walking stiffly, yet not without grace; his gait was the hesitating gait of one who would disguise the fact that, inwardly, he is running away'.[65] Spinell's reaction to his encounter with Klöterjahn junior confirms the moral of the story: what the decadent 'artistic' consciousness is unable to deal with is not banality or the platitudinous, but health and those who exhibit a self-confidence about their place in the world. Artistic achievement, in such cases, becomes not a triumph over weakness, but an excuse for its existence.

*Tristan* is Mann's most succinct exploration of the apparently irreconcilable conflict between the principles of life and consciousness, extroversion and introversion, in short, between the bourgeois and the artist. The gap between these various realms remains unbridgeable in Mann's work until the final story in this series of early novella: *Tonio Kröger*. Seen within the context of Mann's earlier artist stories, *Tonio Kröger* marks a unique attempt to bring together two worlds and two values systems that had confronted one another in bitter hostility. The eponymous hero of that story learns to move across the realms of the artistic and the bourgeois in a way that avoids not only the tragedy of little Herr Friedemann (whose desire to possess the loved one was doomed from its very inception) but also the impasse reached by Thomas Buddenbrook (whose occupancy of both worlds was only sustainable through an exertion of will that was, ultimately, self-destructive). *Tonio Kröger* is the most complete embodiment of a suggestion that briefly surfaced in the conclusion to 'At the Prophet's': art must take to itself a new

respect for life if it is to avoid the charlatanry and inauthenticity
that is part of its very essence. Such sentiments were first voiced
in an earlier story, 'The Hungry'. Its main protagonist (yet
another Detlef) is the typical artist hero of the early Mann:
alienated, hyper-sensitive, introspective and convinced of the
loneliness of his vocation. What sets him apart from types such
as Hanno Buddenbrook and his namesake in *Tristan* is a
passionate longing to belong to the world of middle-class normalcy. His heart-felt exposition of his plight reads like a motto
for the later full-length treatment of a similar predicament in
*Tonio Kröger*: 'We isolated dreamers, disinherited of life, who
spend our introspective days remote in an artificial, icy air and
spread abroad a cold breath as from strange regions so soon as
we come among living human beings and they see our brows
marked with the sign of knowledge and of fear; we poor ghosts of
life, who are met with an embarrassed glance and left to
ourselves as soon as possible, that our hollow and knowledgeable
eye may not blight all joy ... we all cherish a hidden and
unappeased yearning for the harmless, simple, and real in life;
for a little friendly, devoted, familiar human happiness'.[66]

Detlef's *cri de coeur* anticipates an important change that was
soon to take place in Mann's life. By the time of the publication
of *Tonio Kröger* in 1903, Mann was beginning to establish
himself as a young and up-and-coming author, capable of
holding artistic self-consciousness at arm's length for the sake of
his chosen craft. He had come to appreciate the benefits of
bourgeois society. There is much that is autobiographical in
*Tonio Kröger*, from the location of the story and Tonio's family
background through to the development of his artisitic career,
and the position of compromise he reaches with the impositions
and limitations of bourgeois society. There are similarities
between life and text even in details of Tonio's physique and
temperament: from his exotic southern mother he has inherited
the brunette face with its 'dark eyes, with delicate shadows and
too heavy lids', and a propensity towards dreaminess and an
inclination to dwell in those places 'where life becomes complex
and dreamy', through to his melancholy introspection and
ability to make contact with the 'power of intellect ('des
Geistes'), the power of the Word, that lords it over the unconscious and inarticulate'.[67] These 'gifts' (that the youthful
Tonio recognizes are of dubious benefit to his future happiness)
mark him off from those, such as the blond blue-eyed Hans

Hansen and his female equivalent, Ingeborg Holm, who occupy the sunny world of normal society, entirely devoted to the uncomplicated action and extrovert behaviour. Ingeborg's grace and agility on the dance floor is a perfect symbol for the self-confidence that she brings to her place in the world, a self-confidence that is so starkly juxtaposed to the gauche and ungainly Tonio. The sphere of self-expression to which Inge and Hans are drawn is that of the body, whilst Tonio is drawn to the mind, and in spite of the self-abnegation and humility that Tonio feels towards this world, he is forced to recognize that he, as the artist in the making, can never belong to it.

By the time we reach the second part of the story, we have arrived at the familiar point in Mann's early stories where the hero is determined to register his alienation from the world in terms of his identity as an artist. Now an adult, with some success behind him, Tonio has become, like so many of the Mannian artist figures before him, 'fastidious, precious, *raffiné*, morbidly sensitive in questions of tact and taste, rasped by the banal'.[68] Tonio has also acquired the credo that goes with this decadent artistic sensibility, a vision of his vocation as a 'curse', the product of an almost criminal disregard for the conventions of middle-class society. In conversation with his soul-mate, the Russian painter, Liseweta, he speculates upon his condition: 'Only the irritations and icy ecstasies of the artist's corrupted nervous system are artistic. The artist must be unhuman, extra-human; he must stand in a queer aloof relationship to our humanity', because, as he later elaborates, 'there is a gulf of ironic sensibility, of knowledge, scepticism, disagreement between [the artist] and the others'.[69]

Tonio's self-image does not, at first sight, seem an advance on that nurtured by his forerunner, the aesthete and celebrant of sickness, Detlev Spinell in *Tristan*. Both assume that creativity, knowledge and irony are irreconcilable with the values of the bourgeois world. But whereas Spinell is more than happy to accept the terms of this equation and the irrevocability of the gap between the artistic and the bourgeois, Tonio, through the example and arguments of his companion, admits to a residual feeling of dissatisfaction with this image of the alienated artist. In spite of the theory, Tonio has retained that longing for 'life, in all its seductive banality' which he had experienced with an almost erotic intensity during his boyhood infatuation with 'the blue eyed ones' in his home town. In spite of efforts to fully embrace the credo of aestheticism, Tonio has remained in Lisaweta's succinct phrase a 'bourgeois on the wrong path, a bourgeois *manqué*' ('ein verirrter Bürger').[70]

In an effort to regain contact with this world, Tonio undertakes a visit to his home town where he first experienced his sense of alienation. He finds much changed in the physical identity of the city, notably his former ancestral home, which is now a library. But the greater and more significant changes have occurred within himself; the years of dedication to the muse have produced in him a sureness of self-image and self-confidence that allows him to dispense with the sense of identity that his birthplace provided. Tonio no longer needs to feel a part of this world; he can choose where to belong and to whom to belong. Even his detention by the hotel manager on suspicion of being a 'swindler' cannot shake his sense of identity (indeed, on a comically ironic note, Tonio is happy to admit that he is, like the wanted criminal, of 'unknown parentage and unspecified means', and the perpetrator of 'shady transactions').[71]

Tonio survives, thus, his first test; the second is posed by his meeting with Hans and Inge, now a married couple, whom he encounters on an expedition to a coastal resort in Denmark. The episode confronts Tonio once again with all the components from his youth that were responsible for his original sense of alienation: the blond, blue-eyed physicality of the protagonists, their sense of poise and self-confidence expressed through dance, their natural bonhomie and uncomplicated sense of fun, which makes them in Tonio's eyes representatives of 'the pure, the blithe, the untroubled in life'. And, as before, he is forced to remain an outsider in their company, looking on, in an almost voyeuristic way, at their merry-making, with a mixture of feelings that even he cannot fathom: 'longing? tenderness? envy? self-contempt?'.[72] The reconciliation that both Tonio and (by dint of artful manipulation of narrative sympathy) the reader has longed for fails to take place. Tonio remains an outsider in this world. But unlike Detlev Spinell and the other aesthetes before him, Tonio has matured to the point where he realizes that his newly-won feeling of respect and longing for this world cannot be impaired by its rejection of him. It will remain intact, because it has become for him an artistic necessity. In the letter to Liseweta which concludes the novella he takes leave of his former self and outlines an artistic credo that will take him into the future: 'I admire those proud, cold beings who adventure upon the paths of great and demonic beauty and despise "mankind", but I do not envy them. For if anything is capable of making a poet of a literary man, it is my *bourgeois* love of the human, the living, the usual. It is the source of all warmth, goodness, and humour'.[73]

Writing to his close friend, Kurt Martens, three years after the publication of *Tonio Kröger*, Mann called that story a 'confession of love for life which verges on the inartistic in its overtness and directness'.[74] Tonio Kröger's concluding comments certainly represent Mann's greatest attempt to overcome the gap between the artist and society that forms the major theme of his early fiction. But Mann might also have added that the story also expresses a 'confession' for love of a certain type of art or artistic attitude, one that refuses to be seduced by the mystique that surrounds art, but engages willingly with all aspects of the human drama of life. Seen from this point of view, *Tonio Kröger* can be read both as a critique of the aesthetics of decadence and as a personal artistic commitment on Mann's part to a continuing exploration of the human, all too human, realm of the "low-lands" of bourgeois society.

# 4

# *Liebestod: Death in Venice*

The figure of the artist in the early short stories and novella of Thomas Mann proved a perfect vehicle for his exploration into the nature of attenuated sensibility and its problematic relationship with the social world. It was on the basis of this incisive and highly personal engagement with the problem of artistic sensibility that Mann came to be known as one of the great psychological writers of the age.[75] In spite of the sympathy with which the characters in these early stories are depicted, they are, however, subject to a certain ironic perspective which allows us to see the comic as well as the potentially tragic nature of their predicament. This is true even in *Tonio Kröger*, which is by far the most thorough exploration of the gap between artist and society in the works of Mann's early period. Thomas Mann called that story his '*Werther*', because, like Goethe's novel, *Tonio Kröger* is essentially a study of the pain that accompanies a youthful longing for acceptance and recognition by the loved one and by society. Tonio's suffering, in the end, is as much a consequence of his young years as it is of his status as an artist.

It was not until *Death in Venice*, published almost a decade later, in 1912, that Mann was able to give the conflict between the artist and society a greater degree of moral seriousness. *Death in Venice* gives expression to a new vision of artistic psychology, which looks for a definition of its subject not in the naive longing and excessive idealism that characterized Mann's early artistic heroes, but in the personal transgressions committed by its hero, the writer Gustav von Aschenbach. In a letter written in 1923 to Felix Bertaux, Mann said that the story could best be seen as 'Tonio Kröger retold at a later stage in life'.[76] Indeed, in *Death in Venice* we have left the introverted and youthful world occupied by so many of Mann's early heroes and returned to the world of

48

the father, first explored in *Buddenbrooks* over a decade earlier. For in *Death in Venice* we are dealing with an artist standing, not at the beginning of his career and, like Tonio Kröger, unsure of his direction, but at its end, with a body of work achieved, a philosophy of art fully formed and accepted by his society.

The novella begins, in fact, precisely at that point where the artist hero has just received the confirmation of his standing in the community by being ennobled to Gustav *von* Aschenbach. This ennoblement has been made in recognition of Aschenbach's contribution to the official literary culture of his contemporary Germany; for, unlike the many alienated artists in Mann's earlier fiction, Aschenbach most decidedly belongs to the world of respectable bourgeois virtue, 'enjoying among his fellow-citizens the honour which is in rare cases the reward of intellectual eminence'.[77] Aschenbach, indeed, has always belonged to such a world. As the narrator tells us, he was born as 'the son of an upper official in the judicature, and his forbears had all been officers, judges, departmental functionaries – men who had lived their strict, decent, sparing lives in the service of king and state'.[78] From this background, Aschenbach inherits values and attitudes which will later appear in his art: a sense of discipline, concern for form and, above all, a moral resolution that has no time for ambiguity or relativism, but seeks a 'purity, symmetry and simplicity' in its representation of the world. What Aschenbach has set out to create through his literature is a new classicism that will counteract the prevailing modernist tendency of his age, which looks for its truth in a psychological exploration of personality. Aschenbach has given up that direct and immediate contact with life in all its aspects (the 'sympathy with the abyss') to create a literature that is free of irony, ambiguity and introspection, and written purely in the service of formal perfection.[79]

Aschenbach's character and the aesthetic that he espouses fully accords with certain tendencies in the official culture of Wilhelminian Germany. It is no coincidence that his motto, *Durchhalten* ('persevere'), which sums up the 'heroic' self-command necessary to produce such a rarefied art form, was also that of Frederick the Great. For what Aschenbach is producing through his neo-classical art is very much in keeping with the prevailing ideology of the German state, whose rigid values Mann had already identified in *Buddenbrooks* as being an inordinate respect for 'authority, duty, power, service, the career'.[80] Aschenbach has fled from the purely subjective and personal in order to create an art in keeping with the official dictates of the state, and a literature that can be set for a model in the schools.[81]

Mann himself had, in the early years of his career, been precariously close to Aschenbach's position. When Aschenbach is described as having turned his back on the mysteries of literature, '[calling] genius itself into question, [and] taking the breath of the twenty year olds with his cynical utterances on the nature of art and the artistic life', the narrator is alluding to the ironic perspective that the Mann of the *Tristan* period employed in his own discussion of art and the artistic vocation. This was the period during which Mann, following the success of *Buddenbrooks*, was in danger of becoming absorbed into the literary establishment, of becoming a 'safe' writer, producing a literature that would find acceptance amongst his reading public, rather than provoking or unsettling it. In a number of letters written in the period prior to publication of *Death in Venice*, Mann argued that the process of artistic creation was an 'heroic struggle' which required exertion, will-power and the capacity for self-sacrifice. Writing to his close friend, Kurt Martens, in 1906, he summed up his position in words that would later be echoed by Aschenbach: 'I am an ascetic insofar as my "conscience" directs me towards "achievement" (Leistung) in contrast to pleasure and "happiness"'.[82]

*Death in Venice* emerges, then, out of a process of self-criticism: it explores the consequences for the physical and psychic health of the artist of this 'heroic' attitude to his vocation. Aschenbach becomes, like his favourite character, Saint Sebastian, a martyr to his vocation as a public figure, and to the strictures of artistic performance that position him permanently labouring 'at the edge of exhaustion'.[83] His 'achievements' are made possible only through the imposition of a personal regime of self-abnegation that leads to a withering of his essential life forces, from whose meagre reserves he attempts, 'heroically', to create. Like Thomas Buddenbrook before him, Gustav von Aschenbach survives solely through a philosophy of self control that is symbolized in one of his typical bodily gestures, that of the clenched fist. Mann takes the concept of the triumph of the will from his mentor, Friedrich Nietzsche; but as Mann had already shown in *Buddenbrooks*, assertiveness which grows out of an attempt to hide its lack of natural strength is the wrong type of Nietzscheanism, a caricature of a philosophy that argues for the individual's right to impose himself upon the world, but thoroughly condemns all propensities to self-delusion. What Nietzsche argued for in life, as in art, was, in fact, a balance of the two psychic forces within the individual, which he identified with the gods of Greek mythology: Apollo and Dionysus. The former is the representative of order, discipline and tranquillity; the latter stands for brute energy, chaos, the rapturous, those psychic dispositions which surface in 'endemic trances, collective visions and hallucinations'. According to Nietzsche, art 'owes its continuous evolution to the Apollonian-Dionysian duality, even as the propagation of their species depends on the duality of the sexes, their constant conflicts and periodic acts of reconciliation'.[84]

Aschenbach is an artist who, in an attempt to produce an officially acceptable classicism, has ignored the needs of the Dionysian in his art, as he has repressed the sensuous and hedonistic in his life. What *Death in Venice* charts is the return of these elements, 'so strangely metamorphosed' into harbingers not of a productive regaining of contact with body and health, but of a fateful eruption of excess and intoxication that will carry Aschenbach across the boundaries of the 'normal' into a world of transgression and death. It is highly significant that this experience takes place in the Italian city of Venice, which had long exerted a peculiar fascination on German artists and philosophers: both Nietzsche and the poet August Graf had composed poems extolling the city's morbid charms, and Aschenbach recollects, with 'mingled emotions of joy and suffering', the words of the latter's verse as he prepares to disembark in Venice; above all, it was in Venice that Wagner had completed his opera *Tristan und Isolde*, a work that evokes in its famous 'Liebestod' scene precisely that fatal combination of erotic allure and self-abandonment to which Aschenbach surrenders in *Death in Venice*. Mann was fully aware of its symbolism when he himself visited Venice in 1911: it is a city of fateful ambiguity, the perfect image of the coexistence of classical grandeur and decay, of (in the words of the novella) 'splendid marble arches' that are encompassed by the 'faintly rotten scent of swamp and sea'.[85]

What compels Aschenbach to leave his native town for such an exotic destination is the awakening of a 'vaulting unrest' that he discovers within himself during one of his constitutional strolls through the streets of Munich. That this feeling is something much more radical and much more ominous than a traditional *Wanderlust* is recognized immediately by the narrator who describes it as 'a seizure, almost a hallucination' ('zur Sinnestäuschung gesteigert').[86] Mann was later to describe this violent feeling within Aschenbach as an invasion of the 'Erotic-Dionysian', and, indeed, there is more than a suggestion that what is being reawakened here is a specifically sexual instinct.[87] The 'widening of the inward barriers' which Aschenbach experiences culminates in a vision of exotic and hypertrophic nature: 'He beheld a landscape, a tropical marshland, beneath a reeking sky, steaming, monstrous, rank – a kind of primeval wilderness – world of islands, morasses, and alluvial channels. Hairy palm-trunks rose near and far out of lush bracken and fern, out of bottoms of crass vegetation, fat, swollen, thick with incredible bloom'.[88] The passage strikingly combines images of over-ripeness and hypertrophy with a sense of decay and disorder and, as such, anticipates the malaise to which Aschenbach will eventually succumb. The sinister connotations of Aschenbach's primeval seizure only become clear, however, with the appearance of the solitary 'pilgrim' figure. His first sighting is, significantly, opposite a graveyard, in a stonemason's site occupied by amongst other things, a 'mortuary chapel'. With his rucksack and crook, this uncanny character is himself dressed for a journey; but his ruthless countenance, exotic colouring and empty stare suggest that his presence is an ominous one. It is not, however, until later in the novella, when the traits of this character reappear in two other figures at moments of crisis in the story, that the reader is able retrospectively to establish the identity of this apparition: he is a Hermes figure whose hypnotic gaze upon Aschenbach portends a community of spirit between the two: in death.

The first part of *Death in Venice* gives the reader warning that the energies reawakening within Aschenbach are linked to an excess of instinct that will have, not life, but death as its resolution. Even on the journey to his destination, the 'Hotel des Bains' on the Venetian Lido, the ominous nature of Aschenbach's journey is underlined by his encounter with two characters: the garishly clad 'young-old man' on the steamship (whose investment in appearance for the sake of attracting the local youths anticipates the development of Aschenbach's own proclivities later in the story); and the mysterious gondolier, who offers to transport Aschenbach in the coffin-like gondola from the landing-stage to the hotel. The latter incident is of particular importance, for it introduces a new note into Aschenbach's plight: self-surrender. For, once he has boarded this sombre craft, Aschenbach finds that he no longer has the will to resist the deviant path of the gondolier, who sets his course not landwards, but out towards the open sea: 'Alone on the water with this tongue-tied, obstinate, uncanny man, he saw no way of enforcing his will. And if only he did not excite himself, how pleasantly he might rest! Had he not wished the voyage might last forever? The wisest thing – and how much the pleasantest! – was to let matters take their own course. A spell of indolence was upon him; it came from the chair he sat in – this low, black-upholstered arm chair, so gently rocked at the hands of the despotic boatman in his rear'.[89]

What has taken place so far in the story has remained within the subjective realm of Aschenbach's consciousness: the characters he has met, the experiences he has undergone have been largely the product of feeling, phantasy and premonition. Even the spectral characters that he has encountered in his journey to Venice seem to occupy a middle-ground between dream and reality, between Aschenbach's imagination and fact. It is only with the appearance of the strikingly handsome young Polish boy, Tadzio (whose family are likewise guests of the hotel) that the radical psychic changes that are taking place within Aschenbach can find an objective focus. A number of heroes in Mann's early stories before *Death in Venice* had also felt attracted to the male body. The adolescent hero of *Tonio Kröger*, for example, does not attempt to hide the fact that his 'love' for Hans Hansen is based largely upon physical attraction to the latter, whom he sees as 'uncommonly handsome and well built, broad in the shoulders and narrow in the hips, with keen, far apart blue eyes'. It is an adolescent infatuation that is overcome, the story implies, by Tonio's later, and more 'normal', preoccupation with the blond Inge. And yet a certain amount of illicit desire remains in his attitude to Hans Hansen. When Tonio does finally regain contact with him at the Danish sea resort, the latter is, unlike Inge, who is now his wife, unchanged, and is still wearing what appears to be the same coy sailor's outfit that he wore during his school days, and has retained the same boyish physique. It is an experience that gives rise to inner turmoil for Tonio, as he steals on tiptoe to a vantage point where he can view without being viewed, his skin prickling 'with the thievish pleasure of standing unseen in the dark and spying on the dancers there in the brightly lighted room'. It is an image of the artist as alienated subject; but it is also a view of Tonio Kröger as voyeur.[90]

*Death in Venice* brings to the surface the element of eroticism that had existed purely in the margins of *Tonio Kröger*. Aschenbach possesses, in his attraction towards the blond and blue-eyed Tadzio, the same combination of bad conscience and sense of superiority that Tonio Kröger felt towards his loved one. But the mechanisms that Aschenbach uses to dissimulate and ennoble his infatuation are immeasurably more complex. In keeping with the formalist aesthetic to which he has adhered throughout his life, Aschenbach construes his feelings towards the boy in terms of a purely disinterested appreciation of abstract beauty: Tadzio is likened unto a Greek sculpture, whose perfect beauty possesses a 'chaste perfection of form' which exudes 'self-respecting dignity, discipline and sense of duty', representing precisely the Apollonian ethos that Aschenbach had espoused prior to the 'invasion' of psychic forces described in the opening section of the novella. It is, then, to 'transcendent matters' relating to the good and the beautiful, rather than to those of corporeality, that Aschenbach turns to make sense of his growing interest in the boy.

Aschenbach's attempts to provide an aesthetic justification for his growing infatuation with Tadzio lead him (and the narrator) into an elaborate discourse upon the nature of beauty and upon the relationship between morality and form. There is good reason to believe that Mann himself sympathized with Aschenbach's plight, both from a personal and professional point of view. Writing almost a decade later, he identified Aschenbach's plight as one experienced by all artists who seek a 'dignity' in their calling: they seek the good and the beautiful, but can only reach these through the senses, through seeing the general ideal of beauty established in its particular physical form.[91] This is exactly how Aschenbach sees his predicament, which he tries to make sense of in terms of Plato's discussion of the problem in one of the latter's Socratic dialogues: the *Phaedrus*. Aschenbach's commentary on the classical story allows the reader to speculate upon the aesthetic implications of his infatuation, to see it, so to speak, *sub species aeternitatis*, as a timeless conundrum for the lover of art, purely 'a puzzle of the artist nature' which, caught between 'licence and discipline' ('von Zucht und Zügellosigkeit'), wishes to appreciate physical beauty without succumbing to the grossness of desire.[92] Thus viewed, it is a noble goal, in spite of the inevitability of its failure. It also has the added consequence of making Aschenbach the *object* not the *subject* of this liaison; he is a victim of a universal predicament. It is in such a light that Aschenbach represents the situation to himself, and to the reader, who is encouraged to see matters in similar terms during those episodes in which the narrator adopts, for the sake of psychological effect, Aschenbach's perspective.

There are good reasons to believe, however, that the elaborate aesthetic speculations and the extended Antic references have another function to perform: they are ways of dissimulating the less noble nature of his attraction for the boy, to hide the fact that the ultimate goal is not appreciation but possession. This becomes clearer as the plot develops, but it is anticipated by the narrator whose frequent references to the presence of disease in the immediate environment contrast starkly with Aschenbach's idealist construction of his infatuation with the boy.

Disease and beauty have, in fact, been associated as themes from the very first stages of Aschenbach's attraction to the boy. Even when the latter is first introduced, Aschenbach's enthusiastic and highly idealist descriptions about Tadzio's 'God-like' form are ironically undermined by the narrator's references to the 'stagnant odour of the lagoons' which accompany this aesthetic appreciation.[93] As Aschenbach's infatuation with the loved one grows into an obsession, the nature of this disease becomes increasingly clearer, until it is finally realized (even by Aschenbach) that the whole area is seriously infected, and that to remain in Venice will seriously endanger his health. Aschenbach now undergoes a bitter internal conflict between 'inclination and capacity', between his desire to remain in the presence of the loved one and his ability to undertake what he knows to be the wisest and safest course of action. His failure to do the latter (caused partly by the 'accident' of a piece of misdirected luggage) marks the beginning of the end for the Apollonian persona that he has so far successfully retained. By the time that he resumes his appreciation of Tadzio's antics on the beach, it is clear that he has abandond his earlier high principles.

*Thomas Mann*

Aschenbach has become one with his new environment: both Venice and the poet are hiding an inner corruption; in the case of the former, a life-threatening choleric disease (which exists behind the splendour of its classical façades), and in the case of the latter, a homo-erotic obsession with the boy (which is obscured by a discourse on aesthetics). As the narrator concludes: 'the city's evil secret mingled with the one in the depths of his heart'.[94]

Even the temporary obfuscation of these states of corruption involves the construction of an elaborate process of false artistry on behalf of both the Italian authorities and Aschenbach alike. The lies and false information put out by the former to hide from the tourists the truth about the bad vapours which come to infect the resort are more than matched by the self-deception, evasion and general loss of dignity that Aschenbach, who has become less and less 'disposed to self-analysis', willingly embraces.[95] To objectify this latest dimension of Aschenbach's decline, Mann introduces yet a further character: the 'baritone buffo' street singer, who turns up one evening to entertain the hotel guests with his songs and lewd humour. The street singer acts as a linking character in the novella, bringing together the sinister Hermes figure of the early section (with his outlandish physique and physiognomy) with the garish old-young character who 'befriends' the local youths on the steamer. The themes of death and illicit sexuality are combined here, and in the form of a caricatured and obscene version of Aschenbach's own calling: that of the artist. Like Aschenbach, so too this 'performer' creates his work out of a mixture of 'defiance and self-will', and is dependent upon a public for acclaim and sustenance.[96] But also like Aschenbach, the singer has overstepped the 'physical distance' between himself and the respectable world, as he attempts to wheedle himself into the affections of his audience. Finally, with his garish make-up the buffoon looks forward to what Aschenbach will become once he is entirely in the grip of his infatuation. Then he will undergo a series of cosmetic treatments in the hope of creating the impression of youthfulness, an attempt at 'artistry' that sums up the fallacious credo that he has adhered to throughout his life: the belief that appearance can, through an act of will, be imposed on an inner life, however empty or exhausted that might be.

The street singer signals yet a further theme: that of the

abandonment of restraint and self-control. For what is even more demeaning than the semi-obscene cabaret that Aschenbach is subjected to is his realization that he is unable to break its 'spell', that he is prepared to tolerate humiliation for the sake of the as yet undefined 'boons that chaos might confer'.[97] He is also prepared to tolerate losing his life in what he now knows, following his visit to the English travel agent, to be an incipient cholera epidemic. In order to quench his 'madness of desire', Aschenbach is prepared to risk everything: life, reputation, public honour and self-respect, indeed, his very identity as a moralist, on which he prided himself so greatly. It is this realization (at one and the same time 'triumphant' and 'sickening') that initiates the final stage in his downfall. The previous heroic pose of the lover as artistic connoisseur can now be dropped and recognized for what it always was: purely a façade, behind which emptiness and, finally, disease has dwelt. Once the last line of resistance is removed, those Dionysian forces long banished from Aschenbach's life and work can return, and this they do, fittingly, in a dream that (the reader now realizes) has been anticipated from the very earliest pages of the novella. The dream represents a compression, a concatenation of Aschenbach's experiences to date: Tadzio's presence is indicated by the 'long drawn u-sound' with which his name ended, and in the reference to the 'stranger God'. The latter is also reminiscent of Tadzio's 'God-like' form, but also of the sinister figure who appeared in Munich. All are enjoined in a saturnalia of orgy and violence, presided over by the sexual deity of the phallus, 'the symbol of the god-head, monstrous and wooden'. Abandoning the austere and puritanical values that he has held to throughout his life, Aschenbach now throws himself into this celebration of licentious excess, tasting in his very soul 'the bestial degradation of his fall'.[98]

Aschenbach's dream represents a resolution (however imagined) of that longing within the hero that has pressed for recognition throughout his stay in Venice. Had Mann concluded his story at this point, where lover and loved one, desire and the object of attraction reach a symbolic consummation, his fate might have been granted a certain tragic dignity. But it is not on a note of exaltation that Aschenbach is granted his exit, but rather on one of banality. Aschenbach must drain the dregs of his inauthentic life and philosophy. It is not the noble genre of tragedy but that hybrid form of doubtful status, tragi-comedy, that provides the medium for his valediction. Aschenbach will recover from his dream, don his new manikin appearance and furtively prowl the streets of cholera-infected Venice in search of a glimpse of the youthful loved one. And, like a puppet, he will sit, on the very eve of his death, through the consumption of cholera-infected over-ripe fruit, to learn the lesson that he has ignored: that the artist cannot escape the sensual in his life and work; the world must be experienced in full; attempts to adopt Olympian positions are pretence and folly; and, finally, the artist cannot and should not pretend to be a moralist and an educator of youth, for the artistic vocation leads not to edification and sobriety, but to 'the bottomless pit' of excess and transgression. Whether Aschenbach is fully capable of registering this lesson on the limits of the artistic vocation is not made clear. He returns from his walk through the streets of Venice to take up his familiar position in his deck chair by the sea. No longer capable of forming his experiences through speech, he is reduced to the passive appreciation of the gaze, as he sits transfixed, staring, initially at the love-one at play, then, as death approaches, at the formless expanse of the sea, becoming in the end entirely the victim of his obsession.

Thomas Mann called his novella 'the late work of an epoch, on which the uncertain lights of a new era are falling'.[99] The early pages of the novella establish Aschenbach as a writer who has emerged from a distinctly German environment, as someone who has drawn upon the values of his Prussian and Protestant background in order to adapt himself to the needs of the official state culture of Wilhelminian Germany. The failings of Aschenbach's life and personality, his refusal to compromise his formally perfect and 'chaste' art by engaging with the 'abyss' of psychological scrutiny, reflect the impersonal cultural ethos of a society that (as Nietzsche had observed) had displaced sensibility for the sake of political, economic and military achievement. The particular inflection of Aschenbach's predicament has, then, its uniquely German origins.

But while the sources of his crisis may lie within the specific cultural context of his contemporary Germany, their ramifications far exceed the confines of his homeland, to include (as Mann himself noted) the whole of the European continent. The connection between the ailing artist and this wider context are established both by the international setting of the story, and the Italian, Polish, Russian and English protagonists who circulate in it, but also (and more ominously) by the reference to diplomatic tensions made on the very first page.[100] These allusions to the Moroccan crisis of 1911 serve to inject a note of anxiety into the story that is only heightened by Aschenbach's subsequent experiences. Both the critical nature of his experiences and their context suggest that the conventional wisdom and values of late nineteenth-century society are no longer capable of holding in check the emergence of new forces both within the individual but also in history at large; that, in short, Aschenbach's restlessness, his surrender to unmanageable psychic forces and his propensity to self-deception are part of a subterranean crisis that will leave European culture (as it leaves the ageing artist) staring out into the void. When viewed within this wider context, *Death in Venice* can be read as a symbolic reconstruction of the malaise besetting European culture on the eve of the catastrophe of the First World War.

# 5

# Sickness, Knowledge and the Formation of Self: *The Magic Mountain*

The experience of death is central to all of Mann's early fiction, from *Buddenbrooks* (1901) to *Death in Venice* (1912). *Tonio Kröger* is the only major work of this period in which that experience is absent; in all of Mann's other works, death appears either as a brute reality, the inevitable culmination of physical decline, or, more metaphysically, as the object of longing, a solution to the crisis of alienated sensibility that besets many of Mann's early 'heroes', from little Herr Friedemann (in the short story of the same name) through to Hanno Buddenbrook. To a large extent, this preoccupation with death arises quite logically out of the themes that Mann addressed in this early body of work: the relationship between knowledge and sickness, between attenuated sensibility and decadence and the plight of the artist torn between bourgeois happiness and artistic vocation. These are themes that belonged to the artistic generation of *fin de siècle* Europe who seemed to live permanently in repudiation of the comfortable securities of life, and in admiration of all forms of transcendence, including the ultimate one. Indeed, Mann himself, as a young man, had not been impervious to the idealism of longing that characterized the otherworldly temperaments of his generation; nor had he been a stranger to the experience of death as a fact of family life, as is evident in his sensitive treatment of the subject in *Buddenbrooks*.

Throughout these early works, Mann leaves the reader in little doubt that whilst the nature of this longing for death may be noble, being (as its frequent association with music suggests) a precondition for artistic depth, its physical reality is often brutal and far from noble. Mann takes pains to undermine the romantic aura surrounding death, both by describing its process in sobering naturalistic detail (as is the case with the death of Hanno Buddenbrook), and by deflating it, in an ironic fashion, from within, as he does in his depiction of the death of Thomas Buddenbrook, whose Schopenhauerian yearning for transcendence culminates in the bathos of the fatal attack precipitated by a broken tooth.

Death represents, then, an ominous attraction that must be resisted; but not ignored. This is Gustav von Aschenbach's fatal flaw; for the sake of producing a new classicism in his art, that artist banishes from his life as from his work that psychological honesty and essential openness to experience that makes health possible. Repression of the signs of disease and of the growth of a death wish is not the way to health either for the individual or for a society; as Nietzsche had argued, the path towards health lies in recognizing decadence and in overcoming it. Thomas Mann himself, writing in 1925, put it in the following way: 'One can come to appreciate life in two ways. The first way is robust and entirely naive, and knows nothing of death; the other way is familiar with death. I believe that it is only the latter that has any intellectual value. This is the way chosen by artists, poets and writers'.[101]

If the experience of death is a necessary stage along the road to knowledge, from innocence to maturity, the fundamental question arises: 'how can the individual be close to death without belonging to it?' It is this problem that Mann explored in his longest and, for many readers, his most intellectually challenging novel, *The Magic Mountain*, which he began as a short story in 1913, before completing it as a two volume novel in 1924. The enigmatic title refers to the 'Berghof', a Swiss sanatorium where the hero of the novel, Hans Castorp, has come to visit his cousin, who is convalescing from a tubercular illness. Intending to stay for three weeks, Castorp remains for seven years, held in awe by the larger than life characters who inhabit this magic realm of the privileged, and fascinated by the ever-near presence of death. It is here, in an apparently timeless world dominated by habit and a regime of bodily obsession, that Castorp, the blond young engineer, undertakes a journey of intellectual and moral discovery, moving, 'in a comically sinister way, through the

*Thomas Mann*

spiritual oppositions of humanism and romanticism, progress and reaction, health and sickness'.[102]

In undertaking this 'journey', Castorp also succeeds in over-coming certain propensities within himself. For Castorp, like so many of Mann's heroes, is a *Bürger manqué*, caught, like Thomas and Hanno Buddenbrook before him, between a recognition of the importance of the patrician values of family, tradition and the work ethic, and a realization that he is temperamentally and physically unable to live up to such ideals or practise them. As the narrator frequently asserts, Castorp's defining feature is his 'mediocrity' ('Mittelmäßigkeit'), the fact that he belongs neither to the shadowy world occupied by the artist figures of Mann's early fiction, nor quite to that of the blue-eyed *Bürger*, the doyens of healthy unselfconsciousness, who inhabit a world of secure values and moral propriety. What distinguishes him from the latter group is a certain inflection of sensibility (evident in his feeling for music, to whose 'narcotic effect' he regularly gives himself over) and, above all, his early acquaintance with death, which leaves Castorp in a short span of time without mother, father and, finally, grandfather. The process of this familial tragedy is condensed into one short chapter, a narrative technique which serves to highlight the impact of that experience on the impressionable young Castorp, as the ritual and ceremony of death for the loved ones imprints upon the 'still unwritten page' of his sensibility firm impressions of the 'mournful beauty' of death.[103] Standing in front of his grandfather's bier, witnessing a phenomenon that is part noble resolution, part physical decay, Castorp develops (as we learn later) 'a spiritual craving to take suffering and death seriously'.

This feeling for the 'transcendent strangeness' of death is reawakened in the youthful Castorp when he visits his ailing cousin, Joachim Ziemssen. The latter came originally to the sanatorium to seek a cure for a minor ailment, but, like the other dwellers of this 'magic mountain', becomes drawn into the many habits and rituals that constitute its regime of sickness. The sanatorium is much more than a medical institution; it is a self-perpetuating community, with its own laws and customs, goals and values, where a privileged elite remains locked into 'a continuous present, an identity, an everlastingness'.[104] 'Fed up' and 'cynical', the inhabitants of this world, ailing Russian aristocrats, German financiers and English gentility, fill their

lives with a round of petty activities: meals, medical consulta-
tions and parlour games. Even the staff work 'without a real
vocation and burdened with restlessness and ennui' ('von
Langerweile beunruhigt und belastet').[105] The guiding principle
of this community, its *raison d'être*, is sickness. This is evident
not just in the maladies suffered by its inhabitants, but more
concretely in their welcoming of disease as a mark of honour, as
a confirmation of their elect status. The patients of the sanatorium, spurred on by the director, the doyen of the ailing body and
budding psycho-analyst, Hofrat Behrens, are proud of their
illnesses, and talk of their acquisition as a 'talent'. When they
describe the air of the mountains as 'good for illness', the
narrator leaves the ambiguity uncorrected. As Castorp himself
soon notes, up here 'it [is] the sound and healthy person who
[does] not count'.[106]

The sanatorium represents, then, a world set apart from the
normal; it is a 'magic' mountain, inhabited by a privileged clique
who has chosen to flee out of history and into a world hermetically
sealed from the social and political changes that are taking place
in pre-First World War society. But these characters live not
only beyond history; they also exist beyond time, or at least in a
realm characterized by a quite singular notion of time, one that
possesses the 'magical' proportions of circularity and repetition,
where even the seasons fail to follow their conventional chronology.
In such a world, the notion of *objective* time makes no sense; as
Castorp notes, the same unit of time can be both long and short
depending upon how the individual responds to the regime of
habit that dominates the lives of the inmates. The fluidity of time
poses problems for those characters, such as Castorp's cousin,
who still see themselves as part of the normal world of goal-
oriented action and achievement; but for others, such as Castorp, it provides the chance to experiment with established
notions of truth, morality and self.

Castorp is helped along this path of self-discovery by a
number of exceptional individuals. The first is the young
Russian emigrée, Clavdia Chauchat. With her high cheek-bones
and general demeanour, Chauchat reawakens in Castorp long
suppressed sexual stirrings first experienced with his childhood
friend, Pribislav Hippe. Like Hippe, Chauchat possesses eyes of
an ambiguous colour, which speak of the unobtainable and the
illicit.[107] Chauchat is to be an important influence on Castorp,

not because their association culminates in an amorous involvement (she soon leaves the sanatorium to return later in the novel
accompanied by her 'guardian', the charismatic personality,
Pieter Peeperkorn), but because she unlocks something in Castorp's psyche that had lain dormant since his childhood: a
feeling that love and death are somehow equated. Clavdia
Chauchat comes to represent for Castorp that exotic world
beyond the confines of bourgeois existence. Their relationship
culminates in an extended conversation held (in French) during
the carnival celebrations for Shrove Tuesday, when in the aptly
titled chapter 'Walpurgis-Night', Castorp comes to espouse
under her influence a witches' brew of dubious tendencies
centred on the powerful alliance between the body, love and
death. On the eve of her departure from the sanatorium, Castorp
concludes his confession of love for the enigmatic Chauchat with
a testimony to those late-Romantic values that he has since
childhood found irresistible: 'The body, love and death, they
form a unity. For the body, it is both sickness and voluptuous-
ness, and it is this which causes death, yes, both are carnal, love
and death. That is their terror and their great magic'.[108]

This romantic equation is all the more attractive to Castorp
because he has already, by this stage, begun a reassessment of
the value of sickness. Inspired by the example of Herr Albin, a
young man who has renounced all contact with the flat-land below,
Castorp begins to relax his own hold on bourgeois propriety, and,
putting himself in the place of the dissolute and nihilistic Albin,
begins to appreciate 'how it must feel to be finally relieved of the
burden of a respectable life and made free of the infinite realms
of shame' ('bodenlose Vorteile der Schande').[109] The reference
to freedom here needs to be noted, for Castorp's empathy with
Albin is symptomatic of his growing feeling that the regime of
sickness that reigns on the magic mountain can provide the basis
for a personal freedom which, it is implied, is unattainable in the
normal world beyond the sanatorium. Castorp gradually begins
to acclimatize himself to the regime of the sanatorium, accepting
its social customs and surrendering to the various routines that
centre on the care and control of the body. He comes to accept
the habits of the convalescent. Measuring his temperature each
day, he is proud when the mercury rises, and gives himself over
to the comforts of the patients' reclining chair whose 'unanalys-
able, the almost mysterious properties' induce a total feeling of

cocooned passivity.[110] Above all, Castorp now rediscovers that earlier ominous respect for 'death and things connected with death', a recognition which he elaborates into a conviction that seems to signal a final leave-taking from the flat-land of bourgeois values: 'one always has the idea of a stupid man as perfectly healthy and ordinary, and of illness as making one refined and clever and unusual'.[111]

Such sentiments suggest that Castorp has joined those artist figures in Mann's early work who are irretrievably locked into that late-Romantic paradigm of excessive sensibility, erotic sensation, social alienation and a fascination with death. As he finally brings himself to write the letter to his uncle down below, indefinitely extending his stay in the sanatorium, Castorp seems to have reached the end of a familiar line of development for the heroes of Mann's early work; only *Tonio Kröger* ends on a positive note with the hero discovering an irrepressible respect for the world of normal values. But it is a respect that looks for fulfilment in the future, not in the present, and the reader leaves that particular work with a sense of matters incomplete, resolutions as yet unfulfilled. It is to be left to Hans Castorp, the blond young engineer with the faint taint of tuberculosis, to give substance to Tonio Kröger's rather too blithe optimism about the possibilities of reconciling health and knowledge, the bourgeois and the artistic. It is Castorp's task to overcome the Schopenhauerian-inspired pessimism inscribed into Mann's early worldview, and to grope towards the basis of a new humanism. Writing in 1927, Mann outlined the terms of this learning process in the following way: 'The German reaches God by going through the demolition of dogma and the desolation of nihilism; he arrives at the community by first experiencing the depths of loneliness and individualism, and he reaches health only by acquiring final knowledge of sickness and death.'[112]

Castorp is, then, to undergo a formation of self, and break through his affinity with death and sickness into a higher state of being where he can, *on the basis of full experience*, assert the primacy of a humanistic vision of the world. In giving literary substance to this process of formation, Mann drew upon a genre that has traditionally found its greatest exponents amongst German novelists: the *Bildungsroman* ('the novel of personal formation'). The classic works of this genre, which include some of the greatest novels in the German language, such as Goethe's

*Wilhelm Meister's Apprenticeshp* (1796), Adalbert Stifter's *Indian Summer* (1857) and Gottfried Keller's *Green Henry* (1879), trace their heroes' development from individualistic and somewhat naive self-assertion through to acceptance of a broader ethical commitment to their respective societies. Above all, the *Bildungsroman* charts the process of growth and the overcoming of adversity. As the philosopher and literary theorist, Wilhelm Dilthey, noted: 'The dissonances and conflicts of life appear as the necessary growth points through which the individual must pass on his way to maturity and harmony'.[113]

*The Magic Mountain* may be viewed as a *Bildungsroman*, but it is one which registers many departures from the earlier classical models. The context of Hans Castorp's process of self-formation is not society, but the hermetic world of the sanatorium. It is here that he encounters a number of influences, positive and negative. He is first confronted with a series of medical knowledges that pretend to offer an insight into his inner self: psycho-analysis and x-ray photography. Both, quite clearly, use different means to reach different parts of the body, but they have one thing in common: they both attempt to illuminate the 'infected areas' of the patient's inner self, and have, as their natural goal, the discovery of sickness not health. For Hofrat Behrens and his psycho-analytic associate, Dr Krokowski, the 'puzzle of life [is] easier to approach by uncanny, even morbid paths than by the way of health'.[114] The director and his assistant are themselves part of the regime of illness that reigns in the sanatorium, and confirm rather than disrupt Castorp's pre-existing penchant towards morbidity and the romanticizing of death. To overcome this propensity, Castorp must look elsewhere, beyond the realm of the sanatorium.

Ludovico Settembrini is one such influence. Although he too is a patient at the sanatorium, it is significant that he lives apart from that institution, in a village, and closer to the normal world beyond the magic mountain. Settembrini, poet, pedagogue and man of letters, is a fervent critic of the sickly ethos which pervades the sanatorium. Whilst in many external respects a comic figure, Settembrini, by casting Castorp in the role of 'Odysseus in the kingdom of the shades', is the first to alert the reader to the fact that the hero of the novel has embarked not just on a medical cure but a spiritual journey.[115] In his Latin dictum 'placet experiri' ('he desires to experiment'), he provides a neat tag for Castorp's attitude towards his new experiences on the magic mountain. Settembrini is a character rare in Mann's fiction, for he represents a first attempt to define intellectual depth outside of the heritage of ideas left by that constellation of mentors who govern Mann's early work: Schopenhauer, Wagner and Nietzsche. Settembrini is both a rationalist and a humanist, a believer in progress both as a concept but also as a force for political, social, technological and scientific change. He is an advocate of European Enlightenment, and a radical opponent of the varieties of 'darkness', intellectual and moral, that he sees as constituting late-Romantic thought. He endeavours, in a number of far-reaching discussions with Castorp, to dissuade the latter from his growing sympathy with disease, music, death and the body.

Settembrini is, at times, a sententious and bombastic dialectician; but he does have a positive effect upon Castorp who, under his influence, starts to view critically the mystique of illness that is such a powerful presence on the magic mountain. He is on the point of accepting his mentor's ideas when a second powerful intellectual force appears to challenge the humanistic ideals expounded by Settembrini. Leo Naphta, a renegade Jesuit with Marxist leanings, represents a philosophy that completely negates the humanism of Settembrini, and, in a series of intellectual disputations, forces Castorp to reconsider the humanistic philosophy that he is slowly coming to accept. Espousing a philosophy compounded out of medieval scholasticism and late Romanticism, Naphta, in his first two dialogues, turns Settembrini's worldview on its head: not the individual, but the state, not internationalism but nationalism, not freedom but belonging, not the political but the religious, not reason but terror, not self-expression but asceticism constitute the ways that govern the world. Even in his explicitly political views, Naphta rejects the 'bourgeois' heritage of parliamentary democracy and, styling himself as a 'reactionary revolutionist' ('ein[en] Revolutionär der Erhaltung'), embraces a politics that clearly anticipates the fascist models of the state that were to develop in the 1920s and 1930s in Italy and Germany.[116]

As Castorp himself soon realizes, the continuing debates between these two 'opposed spirits' constitutes, in effect, a struggle for his soul. When, after one particularly heated debate, he asks himself 'where lay the true position, the true state of

man?', he can find no answer, because, in spite of his modest
contributions to the disputations between Naphta and Settembrini, Castorp has remained, up to this point in time, a relatively
passive onlooker, and the *object* rather than the *subject* of the
elaborate intellectual dialectic charted in the novel. That position changes quite radically in the chapter titled 'Snow'. Here, in
an attempt to clarify his thoughts regarding all he has learnt and
experienced, Castorp takes himself alone into the 'blinding
chaos' of the treacherous snow-fields a good distance from the
sanatorium. This trip into the snow-fields is much more than a
day outing to clear the head. As the narrator's qualifying
references to 'deathly silence', 'sleep' and the 'unconscious
burden' suggest, Castorp is undertaking a metaphorical journey
into himself, to confront his own fascination with death, 'the
billow, the lion's jaws, and the sea', and to establish, once and
for all, whether he is strong enough to withstand that fascination
when the chance of turning it into a reality finally presents
itself.[117] Castorp's journey takes him 'higher and higher towards
the sky' (glowing with an ethereal blue that was a sign of
dissolution for the German Romantics), and further and further
away from recognizable landmarks and, hence, possible assist-
ance. The journey allows Castorp to take stock of the varied
personal and intellectual influences to which he has been subject
during his stay on the mountain: the well-meaning 'wind bag'
Settembrini, the more sinister figure of Naphta, 'that knife-edged
little Jesuit and Terrorist', and finally Clavdia Chauchat, with
her disturbing likeness to Castorp's boy-hood friend with the
'wolf's eyes'.[118]

Castorp leaves them all behind, as he ventures yet deeper into
a snow storm, deliberately trying to lose himself. It is here, in the
heart of this 'whirling nothingness', that he must confront that
part of himself that wishes to surrender to the 'merciful narcosis'
of the snow, and clarify his relationship with the seductive
philosophy of sickness and death embodied in the ethos of the
sanatorium and given an intellectual footing by the theories of
Naphta. Bemused contemplation now must give way to determined action, one way or the other; he must choose life or death.
To choose the latter would mean a consummation with 'the
bride of the storm', a particular marriage of ailing body and late
Romantic intellect into which a number of Mannian heroes
before him, such as Hanno Buddenbrook and Gustav von

Aschenbach, had, in their different ways, willingly entered, and for which his experiences on the mountain had more than adequately prepared him. To choose the former, the way of life, would mean a new start, or a new regaining of those aspects of his 'unmagic' past, the 'sordid bourgeois view of life' ('schäbige Lebensbürgerlichkeit') that he had come to despise.[119]

Castorp chooses life, and, upon its basis, erects a powerful vision of the future that transcends not only the unthinking health of the flat-land but also the intellectual knowledges encountered on the mountain. Momentarily resting from the exertions brought about by his will to survive in a rare spot of shelter, he experiences a vision of a fecund, southern world inhabited by 'children of the sun' who, forming a community of mutual reverence, seem to have found the perfect compromise between the body and the intellect, between individualism and the community, between austerity and 'reasoned goodness' ('verständige[n] Frömmigkeit').[120] Castorp, the embodiment of *Mittelmäßigkeit*, of 'mediocrity' and 'averageness', has come to find the golden mean between the extremes of Naphta and Settembrini, replacing their dubious influences with a third: that of *Homo Dei*, the lord of counter positions who occupies that privileged place between the dignity and moral seriousness of death and the health and animal nature of life. It is a perception of moral maturity which finds expression in a famous formulation: '*For the sake of goodness and love, man shall let death have no sovereignty over his thoughts*'.[121]

The concluding sections of the 'Snow' chapter mark a high point in Castorp's personal development. As if in recognition of this, Mann accords increasingly less space to the debates between Naphta and Settembrini which follow Castorp's important experience. Incapable of intellectual resolution, their apparently interminable disputations can only be stilled by a violent action that calls into question the validity of their respective philosophies. As if affected by the atmosphere of 'acute irritability' and 'nameless rancour' which becomes increasingly more evident in the sanatorium as Europe heads towards the First World War, Naphta and Settembrini agree on a radical solution to their dialectical impasse. Following one particularly acrimonious debate, where they exchange accusations about the wilful misleading of youth and moral conduct, Naphta challenges Settembrini to a duel. In the tragi-comic

scene that follows, the two antagonists confront one another
at short distance with pistols drawn; Settembrini shoots first
(humanist to the last) in the air; Naphta (the grim anti-humanist)
takes perfect aim, and shoots into his own forehead.

Long before this violent confrontation, Naphta and Settembrini
had been displaced in Castorp's affections by yet a further
personality: Pieter Peeperkorn. With his broad chest and regal
countenance, his irrepressible good humour and gargantuan
appetites, Peeperkorn becomes the final and most vital influence
upon Castorp. Beside the bulk and energy of Peeperkorn, his two
other 'over-vocal mentors' seem like dwarfs, their confusing
disputations an empty rhetoric when compared with the 'leaping
spark of wit' that shines through the admittedly rambling but
nonetheless energizing anecdotes and narratives produced by
the burly Dutchman. What Castorp discovers in Peeperkorn is,
above all, the force of personality; in one of his last conversations
with Settembrini, he explains it in the following way: 'I am
speaking of the mystery of personality, something above either
cleverness or stupidity, and something we all have to take into
account: partly to try to understand it; but partly, where that is
not possible, to be edified by it. You are all for values; but isn't
personality a value too?'.[122]

As the personification of the simple values of humanity which
the latter has so recently discovered, Peeperkorn is an important
messenger of life; but he is not an unambiguous one. In his
imposing corporeality and carnivalistic high spirits, he is in a long
line of larger than life confidants who have regularly appeared in
European fiction since Dickens. And yet, there is more than a
trace of irony in the narrator's treatment of Peeperkorn; for the
burly mentor is, like all who dwell on the magic mountain
(including the enigmatic Clavdia Chauchat, who now makes a
reappearance as his consort) diseased, the victim of a series of
bodily appetites that frequently results in over-indulgence and
intemperance. The 'classic gifts of life' (which he so frequently
espouses in grandiloquent terms) consist almost entirely of
eating and drinking, a fact that the narrator ironically notes at
the very end of one of Peeperkorn's most impassioned speeches:
'"Man is nothing but the organ through which God consum-
mates his marriage with roused and intoxicated life. If man fails
in feeling, it is blasphemy; it is the surrender of His masculinity,
a cosmic catastrophe, an irreconcileable horror –". He drank.'[123]

Peeperkorn's personal philosophy, with its insistence upon the primacy of experiences comes, paradoxically, close to that held by the life-denying Naphta, because it pursues pleasure to a point of intensity where the self loses all sense of its individuality and moral identity. His ending, thus, comes as no surprise; too old, tired and ill to live out his hedonistic ideals to the full, the sensual 'instrument of God's marriage' chooses death in preference to a life of diminishing prowess.

What the episode with Peeperkorn shows is that the cult of personality possesses its own insidious mysticism. On Castorp, it has the effect of undermining much of the rational humanism that Settembrini had instilled in his pupil, as well as reactivating Castorp's susceptibility to the romantic lure of dissolution and loss of self. Quite typically, it is the highly irrational (but, for Mann, quintessentially German) art form, music, which provides the medium through which Castorp can at least partially satisfy such inclinations. Towards the end of his period in the sanatorium, a gramophone is supplied. It opens up a new world for the young Castorp, as he gives himself over to the intoxication of musical transport: 'Forgetfulness held sway, a blessed hush, the innocence of those places where time is not; "slackness" with the best conscience in the world, the very apotheosis of rebuff to the Western world and the world's insensate ardour for the "deed" ('Verneinung des abendländlichen Aktivitätskommandos').[124]

Here, 'after so many years of hermetic-pedagogic discipline, of ascent from one stage of being to another', Castorp uses this musical occasion to reflect upon himself and the world, and the nature of his 'journey'. Just as in the classic *Bildungsroman*, the hero comes to acquire a higher wisdom, which allows him a greater insight into the relationship between self and the world, so in Mann's novel Hans Castorp has reached the point where, through music, he has come into contact with the 'blessed hush' that exists behind the bustle of the world and its intellectual façades. But it is not until Castorp hears a subsequent piece of music, the song 'Am Brunnen vor dem Tore', which opens Schubert's song-cycle, *Der Winterreise*, that he is able to give a name to this new reality with which he feels such an affinity: 'It was death'.[125]

Writing to the Marxist literary critic Ernst Fischer in 1926, barely two years after the publication of *The Magic Mountain*, Mann argued the only way that novel could be regarded as being part of the 'revival of the German *Bildungsroman*' was as a 'parody' of that genre.[126] Such an assessment seems, at first sight, to be born out by Castorp's admission of his fatal attraction to music and to that nebulous metaphysical world that it helps him to see. But is this the same concept of death that had such a negative hold on the young Castorp, seven years before, at the beginning of his stay on the magic mountain? There are signs that it is not; but they are only signs. His comments on the seductive alignment between music and other-worldly longing are certainly reflective and of some sophistication, but so was Aschenbach's elaborate employment of classical Greek philosophy in Mann's earlier novella, *Death In Venice*, which was there intended to hide, from protagonist and reader alike, the far from noble changes taking place in the psychology of that character. As with Aschenbach, so with Castorp: at what point is it possible to establish where the theoretical triumph over desire elides into its rationalization? The reader, following the example provided by the 'Snow' chapter, might well expect the final actions of the hero to provide the answer to the central question posed by the novel: 'what has Castorp actually learnt?'. The narrator not only refuses to solve the enigma, but dismisses its relevance, noting: 'we even confess that it is without great concern we leave the question open'.[127]

Instead of providing a clarification of, or neat resolution to, Castorp's fate, the final chapter of the novel simply adds one more puzzling episode to the enigma of Hans Castorp's 'development'. For our hero has returned to the flat-land of the normal world, not to resume his profession, but to enlist in one of the many volunteer regiments who sacrificed themselves in the hopeless battles on the Western Front in the early years of the First World War. The elaborate and sometimes painful process of intellectual formation that Castorp experienced on the magic mountain, seems, as he moves forward, surrounded by his dead comrades, and singing the same Schubert song that had first reawakened his darkly romantic instincts, about to be undone. And yet, as the heightened language of the narrator in this final episode seems to suggest, all may not be lost. To die in a spirit of determined idealism born out of a feeling for the darker recesses of German Romanticism may, in the final analysis, be all that

Castorp knows; but it is not all that he *has known*. Even if it does appear that Castorp, after an elaborate process of self formation, has come full circle, to embrace what he always was, the memory of the journey that he, and we the readers, have undertaken may remain as a 'dream of love' to be set against the sombre irony of Castorp's ending.[128]

# 6

# The Call to Unreason:
## *Mario and the Magician*

In an interview given by Mann in 1925, the journalist Bernard Guillemin advanced the opinion that Hans Castorp, the hero of Mann's mammoth novel, *The Magic Mountain*, published the year before, 'remains a seeker, never reaching fruition'. Mann, in reply, agreed, adding: 'He is a precursor, who is sacrificed. It was not granted to him to become part of the new concept of humanity. He disappears in the war, but not before he experiences a premonition [of the future]'.[129] The reference here to a premonition is an allusion to one of the central chapters of the novel, where Castorp, in serious danger of losing his life in a snow-storm, resolves to fight not only the harsh conditions in which he finds himself, but also the death-wish growing within him. Once out of this dangerous situation, he commits himself, in an act of brave idealism, to the cause of the living and the principle of humanity.[130] It is an impressive resolution, but one that does not, unfortunately, outlast the story. Within a very hour of his return, the steadfast resolution has begun to fade from memory, and, by the end of the novel, our hero has returned to the flat-land, not to resume work in the land of the living, but to offer his services to the German war effort in what was to become one of the bloodiest military engagements in human history. Castorp, the novel suggests, can anticipate but must, in the final analysis, fall short of any real notion of humanism, because he is intellectually bound by his own time, inextricably part of the pre-war period which Mann satirizes for its lack of purpose and moral character. In a world without time and genuine resolution, to have allowed Castorp to have fully acquired a mature moral perspective would have been an anachronism.[131]

What Castorp could glimpse, but not clearly see, was the progress of his fatherland towards the more humane political ethos that established itself in the form of the Weimar Republic after Germany's defeat in 1918. As became clear in an important speech that Mann gave in 1922, it is this political ethos which forms the *Humanitätsideal* that exists merely as a premonition in *The Magic Mountain*. Entitled 'The German Republic', the speech marked an important step in Mann's political development. In his earlier *Reflections of a Nonpolitical Person*, published in 1918, he had extolled the darker virtues of German culture and defended the apolitical nature of the German mind against attacks from the proponents of Western 'civilisation' (who included his brother, Heinrich). What forced Mann to change his mind and to adopt a more positive stance towards the Western liberal tradition was clear evidence that, with the assassination of the Republican Foreign Minister Walter Rathenau in 1922, the nationalist cause had fallen into the hands of an increasingly violent and reckless group of extremists. 'The German Republic' exhorts its youthful audience to turn their backs on these nationalist extremists and their reactionary politics, and to embrace instead the liberal traditions of freedom, the dignity of the individual and tolerance which were inscribed into the constitution of the new Republic. Such values had, in fact, Mann argued, been anticipated in the nineteenth century by a number of German thinkers, such as the Romantic poet, Novalis. Mann's speech concluded with the enthusiastic assertion that the German, caught between East and West, is someone ideally placed to reconcile the oppositions between a series of extremes: 'aesthetic individualism and the undignified loss of the individual in the general; mysticism and morality, and inwardness and the political'. With a clear allusion to his novel in progress, *The Magic Mountain*, Mann summarizes his argument in words that conjure up the experiences of the hero of that novel, Hans Castorp: 'Humanity . . . is in truth the German medium, a realm of the beautiful and humane of which our best have dreamt . . . Long live the Republic!'.[132]

The speech of 1922 is a lengthy and highly rhetorical piece of writing. Some have found its attempts to yoke that ebullient advocate for mass democracy, Walt Whitman, together with the mystical poet of German Romanticism, Novalis, unconvincing, the work of a so-called *Vernunftsrepublikaner*, of someone who supported the Republic not out of genuine conviction but simply because it was the sole means of re-establishing law and order. No such doubts can, however, attend Mann's second major testimony to the Republic, his speech 'German Address: A Call to Reason'. Delivered in October 1930, hardly a month after the ominous election successes of the Nazi party, this speech constitutes an impassioned defence of Republican politics and the principle of parliamentary democracy. In the face of a resurgence of radical nationalist politics, Mann pleas with his largely middle-class audience to resist the overtures being made (and with increasing success) to the electorate by the Nazi Party, and reject the solutions they offer to the economic crisis besetting the nation; their policies may employ the rhetoric of social and national consensus, but their implementation would mean the end of political liberty. The success of their policies would lead to an 'unleashing of instincts, emancipation of baseness and the dictate of force'.[133]

The speech 'German Address: A Call to Reason' represents, however, more than just a call to action; it also offers an analysis of the techniques employed by the Nazis to reach their goals. The Nazis have won success so far because they have, with great psychological insight and the most sophisticated employment of propaganda techniques, produced a style of politics that thrives on 'wild, confusing effects, [which are] at one and the same time, nervous, enervating and intoxicating'. Their fascist brand of politics cannot be explained simply as a reflex of class allegiance or economic interest; it is also a 'psychic disposition', something that draws upon and appeals to 'unconscious forces' within the individual: fears and insecurities, but also wish-fulfilments and phantasies. It succeeds because it appeals, not to reason, but to the irrational, to unreason. The natural ally of the educated middle-class, Mann concludes, is not the extreme Right but the moderate Left, represented by the Social Democrats, who are the sole bearers of the liberal traditions of freedom and democracy.[134]

Mann's speculations about the mechanics of fascist politics provide an important context for one of his major works of fiction of this period: the novella *Mario and the Magician*, published just prior to the speech in 1930. At first sight, the story seems to have little to do with the contemporary state of German politics, or with politics in general. It tells of how a German family on holiday at an Italian sea-side resort come to be bewitched and then horrified by the exploits of Cipolla, a magician cum hypnotist, during one of his evening performances. *Mario and the Magician* takes up a number of themes common in Mann's work, such as the moral ambiguity of art and the artist and the unbridgeable gulf between artist and society to which this leads, but Mann treats these themes in such a way that they become open to political interpretation. For Cipolla is no ordinary stage magician; he is a highly adept hypnotist, whose total control over his audience is made possible by the existence of exactly the same sorts of physic forces, those 'powers stronger than reason or virtue', that demagogues such as Hitler were able to manipulate. It is for this reason that *Mario the Magician* might well be termed a study in the psychology of fascist politics. Cipolla, the 'magician', stands in the same relation to his audience as the fascist politician stands in relation to the crowd at a political rally: both treat their 'audiences' as the passive objects of an elaborate process of manipulation, and both draw on the same techniques to achieve their nefarious goals: intimidation, bluff, brow beating and a mixed bag of 'artistic' tricks and technical illusionism.

*Mario and the Magician* can, then, be approached as a highly sophisticated piece of political symbolism. The story is set in the Italian sea-side resort, Torre di Venere. It is here that the German narrator and his family have retired to continue their summer vacation, distanced from the hurry and bustle of their original destination, Portoclemente. The subsequent psychological unease that the characters will experience during Cipolla's performance is anticipated by the tense atmosphere of the locality which makes the visitors feel 'uneasy' and 'irritable', producing in them (and the reader) a sense of disquiet and foreboding. This feeling is further heightened by the oppressive and unseasonable heat that prevails in the resort, leaving the northern visitors listless and devoid of energy, a physical state that anticipates the radical loss of will-power that will afflict the narrator and his family later in the story.

The climate is only one source of the oppressiveness associated with Torre di Venere. One further source lies in the intemperate values held by the native population and the aggressive attitude they evince towards their German visitors. Certainly, as is clear from his tone and dismissive attitude to the 'very average humanity' and 'middle-class mob' who surround him, the narrator

harbours many of the traditional prejudices of the Northern
European regarding the honesty and integrity of the Mediterranean peoples. And yet, in his pen sketch of the 'public mood'
prevalent in the resort, which combines exaggerated self-importance and chauvinistic excess with a 'naive misuse of power, [. . .]
injustice, and sycophantic corruption', the anonymous narrator,
for all his social and even ethnic prejudices, provides an essential
glimpse into the populist psychology of fascist Italy. Even
amongst the children playing on the beach, nationalist megalo-
mania is evident in the 'quarrels over flags, disputes about
authority and precedence'.[135] It is a world in which the values of
rational humanism, of tolerance and good sense, seem to have
been forcibly excluded. The incidents which exemplify this are
relatively minor: the hysterical reaction of the hotel management
to a child's cough, or inordinate fuss over a favourite table that
can no longer be reserved. Unlike the great confrontations with
history and myth that Mann will later come to grapple with in
the years of his exile, *Mario and the Magician* stays within a
minor mode, using domestic events as a way of pointing to
serious political and ethical issues in the larger world beyond.

The uproar regarding the scanty attire of the narrator's small
daughter is a case in point. Although the event is trivial in itself,
what happens to the narrator during its unfolding and (most
importantly) his response to the same events, serves to crystalize
the major themes of the novel. Playing on the beach in the
extreme heat, the narrator's eight year-old daughter removes,
with the encouragement of her parents, the upper part of her
bathing garment. This behaviour occasions an outcry from the
local population and its authorities, whose over-reaction to a
harmless peccadillo succeeds in blending the 'emotionalism'
endemic to this area with a bloated sense of 'morality and
discipline' that is a characteristic of the new fascist Italy. The
German family are ridiculed in public, castigated by the authorities and fined. More disturbing, however, than the antics of the
outraged Italian authorities (which hover between comic pomposity and sinister thuggishness) is the reaction of the *pater
familias* to this outcry. Not only does he offer no resistance to
what is a clear case of bureaucratic bullying, but he refuses even
to voice his point of view. His anger remains suppressed, his
indignation expressed merely to himself and to the reader.
Instead of taking the principled course of action and leaving the

resort, the narrator and his family decide to remain, a course of inaction which he ominously justifies by invoking the 'poetic' insight that it is 'indolence that makes us endure uncomfortable situations'.[136]

The episode on the beach anticipates the main event of the story: the attendance by the narrator and his family at an evening performance of magic and illusionist tricks conjured up by the 'travelling virtuoso', the 'Cavaliere' Cipolla. Advertising himself as a *'forzatore, illusionista, prestidigatore'* 'strongman, illusionist, conjurer', Cipolla embodies in a heightened way those elements of the public psyche that the story has already identified: a penchant for the melodramatic and theatrical, expressed through an exaggerated sense of self-importance and rampant chauvinism. Cipolla is no ordinary tin-pot entertainer. Although he is a partial hunch-back, with a dress sense and demeanour which verges on a caricature of the down-at-heels aristocrat (encouraging the narrator to reach for epithets such as 'charlatan', 'mountebank', and 'superannuated circus-director') there is nothing self-deprecatory about his presentation of self. On the contrary, Cipolla evinces an extraordinary degree of self-confidence as, through the elaborate use of his 'magical' wizardry, he subjects one member of the audience after another to the imposition of his charismatic personality.

The political symbolism of Cipolla's act is never far from the surface: like a fascist politician at a rally, the 'magician' deliberately arrives late to heighten suspense, nonchalantly scanning the auditorium, establishing his presence, his face set in an 'arrogant grimace', as he initiates a spectacle that is more like a political meeting or 'patriotic demonstration' ('nationalen Kundgebung') than entertainment.[137] He greets his interlocutors with the fascist salute, and speaks in a personal way about Mussolini (although he has but a passing acquaintance with the latter's brother!). Even his very language is imbued with the political rhetoric of the 're-born' Italy, whose 'greatness' knows no 'ignorance and unenlightenment'.[138]

More relevant to the themes of Mann's story, and more central to the exercise of Cipolla's 'diabolic' gifts are, however, the psychological assumptions that underscore the latter's sense of self and his attitude to the audience: a belief in the primacy of the will and of the susceptibility of the masses to the charismatic personality. These assumptions become evident in his very first 'trick', in which a local youth is humiliated by being made to stick out his tongue in front of the audience, quite involuntarily, an action to which Cipolla adds the following mocking comments: 'You do what you like. Or is it possible you have never done what you liked – or even, maybe, what you didn't like? What somebody else liked, in short? Hark ye, my friend, that might be a pleasant change for you, to divide up the willing and the doing and stop tackling both jobs at once'.[139] Cipolla's offer to the young man (and to the audience at large) that they should accept a 'division of labour' between volition and action captures precisely the type of offer made by fascist governments: if the electorate will renounce the 'burden of voluntary choice' in the political sphere, it will receive compensation in other spheres: economic, social and military. When subsequently Cipolla adds, by way of preparing the audience for yet another 'trick', a denial of the existence of the freedom of the will, 'for a will that aims at its own freedom aims at the unknown', he is simply giving expression to the radical cynicism about the viability of liberal democracy held by the fascist politicians of this period.

The relationship between Cipolla and his audience is one of that between a leader and the led. Although Cipolla pretends (like every fascist politician) that he is joined with his audience in some mystical union, forming with them an 'indissoluble unity' of 'commanding and obeying',[140] the narrator reminds us that the 'achievements' of the performance are only possible on the basis of quite specific techniques of manipulation. Like all demagogues, Cipolla is a good public speaker, with undoubted 'professional skill', and a practised touch that passes for 'intuition' and '"magnetic" transmission'.[141] At the core of his performance, however, lies a talent that has nothing mysterious about it: Cipolla is an expert hypnotist. Far from having its origins in the magical influence of personality, Cipolla's authority over his audience is artificially constructed and sustained, and it is the narrator, once again, who focuses our attention on the two essential props of the performance: Cipolla's whip and his recourse to alcohol. The whip, initially a minor prop, becomes increasingly more evident as the story progresses. It is used whenever Cipolla needs to reinforce a command, to underscore the triumph of his will over the sometimes compliant but more often recalcitrant objects of his attention. With its obvious associations with the mastering of animals, the whip is the perfect symbol of the fascist personality in action. The continual references to his alcoholic habits have, however, a quite different set of connotations. They point to the fabrication of that same personality and its artificiality. As such, they serve to remind the reader that the impression of dynamism and purpose that adheres to the fascist persona is artificial, its charisma the result of grotesque 'artistry' and technical promotion.

Cipolla's elaborate performance is aimed at winning the assent of his spectators, but it is noticeable that, with rare exceptions, he takes care 'not to molest the more select ('vornehmen') portion of his audience'.[142] He turns his attentions, instead, to youths who, like the 'two sturdy young louts', turn out to be illiterate and hence unable to assist in one of his word games and, like the ill-fated Mario himself, come from a working-class background. His evident desire to humiliate such youths has clear homo-erotic origins; Cipolla himself makes constant passing reference to the imputed virility of his victims and their likely success with the local maidens, a fact which prompts the narrator to comment on the physical disparity between the partially crippled Cipolla and the fine physiques of his victims. It is no coincidence that his bloody demise follows his declaration of love for Mario, and the planting of a kiss on the latter's lips. But Cipolla chooses these youths for another reason. In spite of his unlikely appearance and the unsavoury nature of his profession, he is, nevertheless, a recognizable source of authority for his audience. By imposing his will upon the energy and naturally disruptive high spirits of these young men, Cipolla is able to show his 'educated public' (whose interest and respect he has allegedly already won) that he is capable of mastering the 'fighting spirit' that emerges out of these representatives of the people. In short, what Cipolla seeks to control through the exercise of his 'magic' is precisely that area of political life targetted by successive fascist governments in Europe: the 'popular sphere' ('volkstümliche[n] Sphäre').[143] It is for this reason that the audience witnesses Cipolla's exertions with mixed emotions, experiencing a conflict in their assessment of the man and the performance: an interest in the success of his tricks is combined with a desire to witness his humiliation; repulsion for his methods is modified by respect for his achievements.

It is the narrator himself who most directly embodies this

ambivalence. It is in his reaction to and assessment of Cipolla's performance that the political symbolism of the story is further developed. Although we learn little about the narrator's background, we can tell by the tone and style of his narration that he is, like Mann himself, a representative of the educated middle-class, precisely that class that Mann felt to be in danger of succumbing to the allure of National Socialism.[144] The narrator, too, is faced with seduction by the irrational in the shape of Cipolla's 'magic', and his narration of the story is both a description of the effects of that 'magic' and a record of his own ability (or lack of it) to resist such effects.

The events described in the early part of the story indicate that such resistance will not come naturally, and this is confirmed by the cirumstances under which the narrator takes the initial decision to attend Cipolla's performance. Confessing that he has a 'need for diversion', the narrator and *pater familias* '[gives] way' to the entreaties of his children and, against his better judgement, commits his family to the evening's entertainment.[145] Once the 'entertainment' is under way, the narrator traverses the scale of emotions that he witnesses in other members of the audience, from repugnance at Cipolla's appearance and general demeanour through to respect for his imposing sense of self-assurance. The narrator's own position is difficult to establish; his frequent admissions of ignorance about the exact nature of Cipolla's 'tricks' and his allusions to the alien stamp of the Mediterranean mentality serve to undermine his own assessment of the performance. Without a clear attitude of his own, the narrator relays his impressions of Cipolla in terms of snatches of conversation he hears around him, the half suppressed notes of disapproval, but also the more vocal appreciations of the 'magician's' way with language and general professional technique.

It is not until well into the performance that he begins to clarify his own position, as the truth slowly dawns on him that he too has become a victim of Cipolla's "magic". What prompts this process of self-assessment is his patriarchal conscience about keeping his children out of bed, and subjecting them to such an unsavoury spectacle. Torn between fascination and guilt, the narrator uses the latter as the basis for an examination of the former, as he now embarks upon a process of speculation which takes him increasingly further into an analysis of the mechanics of manipulation that is the medium of Cipolla's 'magic'. Witnessing the helpless attempts of others to resist Cipolla's 'diabolic powers', and noting within himself a similar vulnerability, he eventually formulates a general principle that is as applicable to the political sphere as it is to the psychological: 'It is likely that *not* willing is not a practicable state of mind ('wahrscheinlich kann man vom Nichtwollen seelisch nicht leben'); *not* to want to do something may be in the long run a mental content impossible to subsist on. Between not willing a certain thing and not willing at all – in other words, yielding to another person's will – there may lie too small a space for the idea of freedom to squeeze into'.[146]

The narrator has now reached a point where he understands not only the mechanics of Cipolla's 'magic', but the general psychological principle which makes it so successful. As such, his insight reads like a call to reason, an overcoming of the 'drunken abdication of the critical spirit' ('trunkene[n] Auflösung der kritischen Widerstände') that has afflicted the audience throughout the performance, as it had affected the German electorate during Hitler's drive for power.[147] The ethical and political implications of the narrator's insight are clear: the irrational is a potent force in human affairs, too powerful simply to be wished away. To resist it, the individual must actively desire its alternative and hold to that as an ideal. For Mann's readership of 1930, on the eve of a seizure of power through Hitler and his National Socialists, the moral would have been quite unambiguous.

Not so unambiguous, however, are the narrator's actions, subsequent to this insight, in the concluding events of the story. Far from marking a break with his earlier admiration for the 'gifted' Cipolla, the narrator's meditation upon the interdependence of liberty and volition turns out, for him, at least, to be no more than an abstract principle. It may have produced a greater vigilance within him, but it has not undermined his respect for Cipolla, nor shaken his passivity in the face of the latter's 'magic'. As 'the magician' comes to the end of his performance with a demonstration of his ability to subjugate the personality of the young waiter, Mario, the narrator pours scorn on the latter's attempts to resist the charismatic Cipolla: 'After all, obedience was his calling in life; and then, how should a simple lad like him find it within his human capacity to refuse compliance to a man so throned and crowned as Cipolla at that hour?'.[148]

The question, meant rhetorically, is not answered by further speculation but by action; repelled by the 'magician's' advances and painfully aware of his humiliation in the eyes of the audience, Mario takes aim with his pistol to destroy the spirit that has tormented him as it has the audience at large throughout the course of the 'entertainment'. This drastic action brings to the surface the 'rebellion that had been smouldering throughout the evening'. It is the final piece of political symbolism that the story will enact, and it is highly significant that it is the humble waiter Mario, and not the more sophisticated narrator, who has proved able to confront the reign of terror imposed on the audience by Cipolla. The narrator welcomes the latter's demise as a 'liberation', but it is one that he experiences in a purely vicarious fashion, as a passive observer of the final drama of that evening.

*Mario and the Magician* must rank as one of the most perceptive and graphic expositions of the psychology and politics of fascism in European literature, but Mann's treatment of the phenomenon raises as many problems as it settles. For whilst the story ends on a note of release, it is hardly one of resolution. The problem lies with the political symbolism of Mario's action. The young waiter has answered force with force, but in doing so has put into question precisely those values of reasonableness, civility and good sense that the narrator had espoused in the early part of the story. Like Cipolla's whip, Mario's pistol is a symbol of a world irrevocably committed to force and extremity of action. Mann's story gives us no sense of a middle-way between the forms of violence represented by Cipolla and Mario. The only possible mediating figure is the narrator himself, but he is, in many ways, the most problematical character in the whole piece: arrogant and dismissive of his Italian hosts (but ingratiating towards the reader), he is caught between moral outrage and grudging admiration, remaining a passive spectator of the psychological despotism that is enacted before his eyes. His insight into the mechanics of fascist charisma, far from providing an alternative and more positive source of values, seems to underscore, rather than counteract, the inevitable success of the irrational, negating any sense of liberation that the reader might have experienced through the dramatic and violent demise of Cipolla, the 'magician'.

# 7

# Myth and Counter-Myth: The *Joseph* Tetralogy

In November 1929, Thomas Mann heard the news that he was to receive the Nobel Prize for literature. It was only the third time that a German writer had been so honoured, and Mann was understandably delighted by the announcement. In the midst of the celebrations, however, he was forced to observe wryly that his fame with the Swedish Academy seemed to rest solely upon the achievement of *Buddenbrooks*, a novel that he had completed almost a quarter of a century before. Mann did not speculate on the reasons for these apparent reservations regarding his mature work. Had he done so, he might well have recognized not only the intellectually demanding nature of his later fiction, but also a certain pessimism of tone or, at least, an undercutting of optimism that is to be found in such 'death-sympathetic' works as *Death in Venice* and *The Magic Mountain*. In their consistent ironic deflation of ideals, both works seem far from providing the basis for the new *Humanitätsideal* (humanist ideal) that Mann asserted in his essay, 'German Republic' of 1922, was the way forward, both for himself and his nation.

It is clear from *The Magic Mountain* and other works of this period, such as *Mario and the Magician*, that Mann did not expect to find inspiration for such an ideal in the political changes taking place around him in his contemporary Germany. By the time Mann had completed the latter work in 1930, Hitler and his National Socialists had set out on a political course that culminated in their infamous 'seizure of power' three years later. Hitler's accession to power in early 1933 has been aptly described by one contemporary as a 'revolution of nihilism'.[149] The

Nazi Party programme consisted of a series of negative slogans: it was against parliamentary democracy, liberalism, Marxism, Judaism and against 'materialism' and city life, in general. It set up as a contrast to such morally 'corrosive' ('zersetzende') aspects of modern life, the notion of the *Volk*, or racial community, in which resided the essence of a people: its culture, language and, above all, race. The Nazis used the notion of the *Volk* to lend a mystical aura and romantic gloss to a political movement that was propelled by the energy of hatred and a will to destruction. The attempts made by the Nazis to press myth into the service of politics did not, however, escape the notice of their critics, including Thomas Mann: 'The entire National Socialist "movement", including its instigator,' Mann wrote in 1933, 'is a prime example of the German spirit's wallowing in the manure of myth. With its fraudulent timeworn pretension to be a "return", this movement offers a real feast to the Germans' hatred of truth, their lust for everything misty and vaporous'.[150]

As if in search of a positive alternative to the negative myth-making of the Nazis, Mann drew upon a theme from the Old Testament for his next novel: the tetralogy, *Joseph and His Brothers*. Mann began his epic revision of the story of Jacob and Joseph in 1926, but did not complete it until 1943. The novel appeared in four volumes: *The Tales of Jacob* (1933), *Young Joseph* (1934), *Joseph in Egypt* (1936) and *Joseph the Provider* (1943). Although *Joseph and His Brothers* has, like many of his other novels, its origins in a personal experience (in this case Mann's visit to Egypt in early 1925), the inspiration to extend what was originally intended as a relatively modest work into a mammoth narrative of epic proportions came from other impulses. A clue is provided by a letter written to Louise Servicen in 1935, in which Mann asserted that in his Joseph novels he had 'broken with the milieu of the middle class and the individual' and moved into the 'realm of the typical and the mythic'. Behind this move was, he added, a desire to explore the roots of 'man's destiny in general', to give literary expression to, in short, 'a new *humane interest*'.[151]

This ambition to give substance to (what Mann calls in a further letter) the 'underlying myths of humanity', is reflected in the very scale of the Joseph tetralogy. The Biblical source of the novel covers 25 chapters in the Book of Genesis (from Chapter 25, Verse 1 to Chapter 50, Verse 21). Compared to many other episodes narrated in the Old Testament, the story of how Jacob's son, Joseph, cheating attempted fratricide, rises from the position of slave to become one of the most powerful overlords in Egypt, occupies a not inconsiderable space. But in Mann's hands the finely drawn pen-sketch acquires an epic proportion and detailed treatment that makes his Biblical-mythical novel both an elaboration of, and a commentary upon, the original. Not only are the briefest of laconic accounts expanded into thorough descriptions (such as Joseph's 'descent into Egypt', which occupies one line in Genesis 39, but almost one hundred pages in Mann's version), but Mann interlards characters and events from beyond the Biblical account in order to provide essential connecting links in his narrative (such as the story of the incestuous brother-sister pair, Huia and Tuia). The result of this process of 'explanation, qualification and expansion' is a work that makes *Joseph and His Brothers* not only by far the longest of Mann's works, but also one of the most epic novels in German literature.

Mann was quite clear about what he hoped to achieve by such an epic narrative: it was no less than the 'transformation of Tradition into Present as a timeless mystery'.[152] The eponymous hero of the work, Joseph, for example, is regarded by the narrator as an 'almost contemporary', and his ancestors, although lost in time, 'modern human beings', 'men like ourselves'.[153] What comes to the fore in this account of the Joseph story is the *complexity* of human psychology, the fact that man is in possession of a 'double self' ('die Doppelnatur des Menschen'), an indissoluble combination of godlike attributes and free essence with sore enslavement to the baser world'.[154] It is Mann's exploration of this psychological duality that makes the Joseph tetralogy, in spite of its apparently arcane subject matter, a supremely modern work. When, at a later stage, the narrator notes that the obeisances made by Jacob and his kin to a burnt sacrifice contained 'something grisly, yet primaevally, pre-religious sacred ('etwas Ur-Unflätiges, greuelhaft Ältestes und heilig Vorheiliges'), which lay beneath all the civilised layers in the most unregarded, forgotten and ultra-personal depths of their soul', he is drawing the reader's attention to those darker forces of the psyche that have so influenced the course of recent history.[155] It is precisely because the world evoked in the Joseph tetralogy is such a morally ambiguous one that the modern reader can relate to it in a 'bond of sympathy'.[156]

The character who most forcefully embodies this complexity of personality is Joseph himself. As the narrator observes: 'the great certainty guiding his life was belief in the unity of the dual, in the fact of the revolving sphere, the exchangeability of above and below, one turning into the other, and gods becoming men and men gods'.[157] Later in the story he is called by the Pharoah 'a prophet and a rogue', and Joseph does, indeed, like many of Mann's other heroes, combine a number of contradictory traits: the sense of artistry and the self-confidence in rhetoric and style exhibited by Gustav von Aschenbach (in *Death in Venice*) and the 'magician' Cipolla (in *Mario and the Magician*) are combined with the sincerity and innocence found in Hans Castorp (the hero of *The Magic Mountain*). To these personality traits is added a certain amorphous sexuality found in a number of Mann's other characters, such as the confidence man, Felix Krull (who forms the subject of Mann's final novel). Joseph stands at the centre of this world of ambiguous morality. It is his experiences that provide a vehicle for the major themes of the novel, and establish the narrative with a focus that sustains it for more than twelve hundred pages.

These are not, however, the qualities of a static hero. On the contrary, Joseph undergoes a thorough process of change during the course of the novel, a process that makes him one of the great protean heroes of Mann's fiction, and establishes the Joseph tetralogy as the most extended example of the *Bildungsroman* in Mann's entire corpus. We first meet Joseph in a characteristic pose, alone in a garden, 'his faced upturned to the moonlight', caught in the throes of a trance brought about by ritualistic incantation.[158] 'Intoxicated by his own lyric ritual, [and] rapt into a growing unconsciousness', Joseph is closer to the Greek god Dionysus, than to any Biblical personage. The scene is aptly set at night, for Joseph's character, at this stage in its development, lacks clear contour or definition, engrossed as he is in his own highly subjective inner world. Later in the story, he will become famous (and, for some, infamous) on account of his capacity to dream and interpret such dreams and, as if to anticipate the exercise of that faculty, the narrator emphasizes the aesthetic side of his personality: Joseph is a gifted writer, a wit, quick at learning and, above all, an accomplished speaker.

Conscious that these talents are allied to a natural beauty, Joseph is also a supreme narcissus, worshipping himself as if a deity. Although such self-adoration later brings him close to extinction, it is not an entirely negative facet of his personality, for one important consequence of this self-regard is his sense of historical mission: it is Joseph who will carry out the prophesy made in the annals of the Canaan tribe that there will appear a 'child of God' who 'will find favour in the eyes of all and kings shall praise him' and who will become the saviour of his people.[159]

Before that can happen, the unity of self and the world that the young Joseph has conjured into existence through his own beauty and talent must be destroyed, so that it can be rebuilt on firmer ground. His sense of providence must be forced beyond the mere egotism that is the central force at work in his young character, and which is evident in the way he treats those who share his world, particularly his kith and kin. In his attitude to other people, Joseph has much in common with the amoral artists who inhabit Mann's early works, such as Tonio Kröger and Hanno Buddenbrook who likewise cultivate an aloofness from a world that they regard as mundane and banal. If Joseph can be regarded as amoral, however, it is not because he desires to perpetrate evil, but rather because he is indifferent to the personal and moral effect of his behaviour on others. This is well illustrated in the famous episode in which, through a mixture of artful persuasion and emotional blackmail, he acquires the Coat of Many Colours from his duped father, Jacob. But there are other, more serious instances of such egotistical behaviour. He is, for example, quite callous in his indifference to the well being of his brothers, and frequently injures their sense of dignity and self-respect by flaunting his status as favoured son. When, in the dream of sheaves, he symbolically depicts them as his servants, Joseph reaches a state (as he himself later relates) of 'culpable self-confidence', from which he barely recovers. Joseph's fatal flaw is that he is incapable of seeing the self in its social context. It is a defect that prompts the narrator to an apt generalization: 'imagination, the art of divining the emotional life of others – in other words, sympathy – is not only commendable inasmuch as it breaks down the limitations of the ego; it is always an indispensable means of self-preservation. But of these rules Joseph knew nothing. His blissful self-confidence was like that of a spoilt child.'[160]

Joseph must learn to give his aesthetic talents a social conscience and a moral content. He must grow up, and to do this his old self must 'die'. The story of how Joseph's brothers, their patience exhausted by his arrogance, beat him unconscious and throw him into a pit, leaving him for dead, stands at the centre of Mann's account of the story, as it does of the Bible's. It is an episode of crucial symbolic import, for it represents an important transitional moment in Joseph's assessment of himself and his attitude to others. It is only whilst he is lying at the bottom of the pit, scared, hungry, and abject that he is able to embark upon a liberating process of self-enquiry, which has the effect of illuminating 'the dark terror in his soul'.[161] As his feelings pass from distress and remorse to pity for the assailants, Joseph discovers within himself a sense of filial identity and familial responsibility that would have been unthinkable in his earlier 'artistic' phase. It is on the basis of this new self-knowledge that Joseph is 'reborn', and Mann uses the discussion between Joseph's brother, Reuben (who, regretting his murderous action, returns to the pit) and the watchman to establish one of the central concerns of the Joseph tetralogy: the theme of redemption and resurrection. The pit is now an empty 'grave', its occupant in the custody of the Ishmaelite merchants. The watchman responds to Reuben's pained confusion by giving an account of Joseph's experiences in the Pit that looks back to pagan ritual just as it looks forward to Christ's Resurrection in The New Testament: 'I saw a youth descend into the grave in garland and festal garment, and above him they slaughtered a beast of the flock, whose blood they let run down, that it ran all over him and he received it with all his limbs and senses. So when he ascended again he was divine and had won life'.[162]

Joseph's salvation from the pit by the itinerant Ishmaelite merchants, who sell him into bondage in Egypt, leads to a loss of liberty; but it also leads to an increase in his sense of personal mission. He now embarks upon the second period in his life in the service of the Egyptian potentate, Potiphar, entering a 'nether world, to which the pit had been the entrance'.[163] Egypt under the Pharoah Neb-ma-Re offers a society and culture that is the very opposite of the frugal and God-fearing peasant world from which Joseph has come. This is a *fin de siècle* society, hedonistic and sensually self-indulgent. Even its religious observances seem marked by carnality, centred as they are on a motley collection of fertility symbols and sun gods, who, like the deity Re-Horakhte, combine the attributes of the 'animal, human and divine'.[164] Joseph will later, drawing upon his faith in the 'one living God', come to sit in moral judgement upon the 'decorative and detestable folk-customs' that govern this world, but, an aesthete himself, he also is drawn to its diversity and vitality, and eventually comes to respect its achievements, legal, financial and architectural. It is, after all, precisely because Egypt is a decadent or late civilization that its rulers are able to recognize and reward Joseph's many talents, overlooking his foreign background and alien faith for the sake of his wit, erudition and personal charm.

What Joseph learns in Egypt are the benefits of service. The experience of the pit has taught him to see adversity as a challenge, and a necessary stage in God's 'special plans' for him.[165] Being an increasingly essential part of Potiphar's retinue allows Joseph (now called Osarsiph) to become master of the web of human problems and relations that constitutes those spheres of which he had previously been ignorant: the social and the ethical. It is under Potiphar's guidance that Joseph rises through the ranks of the household to a position of prestige and relative power. He learns to master his inclinations and to put his gifts to use in carrying out tasks and duties of benefit to those other than himself. It is, then, all the more ironic that at the very height of his growing maturity, at that point where he has become 'more serious and assured', Joseph, in a way that is typical of the reversal of fortune that characterizes his fate, must descend once again for a second time into the pit. And it is a further irony that his fall this time is brought about not by indulgence but by abstinence, as he withstands, for three long years, the entreaties of his master's wife that they should lie 'head to head and foot to foot'. He is guilty on this occasion not because he has succumbed to temptation, but because he has allowed his 'charm' to get beyond control and upset the social and moral order of which he is a part.[166] Stripped once again of his symbolic outer self (in the form of his robe left in his mistress's boudoir), he faces without complaint his accusers and accepts his punishment.

Joseph's second period in the pit proves to be a transitional point along the path to the third and final stage of his story. It is here, incarcerated in a desert prison at a distant reach from civilization, that he once again turns inwards to take stock of his life, reasserting his confidence in the influence of character upon circumstances and his faith that the events of his life are in step with the 'motions of higher things'.[167] Above all, during this second period in the pit, he rediscovers his earlier gift for the interpretation of dreams. The talent that initially proved his undoing is now, ironically, the source of his salvation, as his success in reading the dreams of two inmates, the Royal butler and his hapless colleague, the baker, is passed on to the youthful new Pharoah, Amenhotep.

It is in the latter's service that Joseph, now a man of 30, comes to fulfil his destiny as provider for the children of Israel. He enters the service of the Pharoah as an interpreter of dreams, but leaves it as overseer of all of Egypt. The key to his successful career lies in the lesson he has learnt regarding the necessity of sympathy as a strategy for survival. He has learnt not to compromise truth exactly, but to recognize its flexibility. Whilst the young Pharoah romantically views Joseph as someone who has 'opened the prison of truth that she may come forth in beauty and light', welcoming his advice and interpretations as semi-divine revelations, it is left to the shrewd mother of the sun-king to observe (towards the end of their first audition) that the 'painfully subtle' Joseph has been so successful in impressing the Pharoah because the former has simply been revealing what the young 'sun-king' already knew. Indeed, the Joseph of this final section of the novel has much in common with his younger self. Earlier, Reuben, his brother, had noted a strange duality in Joseph's character: he was 'malicious in his innocence and innocent in his malice' and this combination of character traits comes to dominate in the final stages in his life. Joseph combines calculation and artlessness, idealism and pragmatism, humour and sincerity, self-adulation and modesty in a way that tends to confirm the Royal assessment of him as 'not only a prophet but a rogue' ('ein[en] Weiser nicht nur, sondern auch ein[en] Schelm').[168]

Such a constellation of ambiguous character traits might well be self-defeating were it not for the fact that they sustain Joseph in his higher mission. Joseph is allowed to be an egotist because the achievement of a higher destiny, one sanctioned by God, requires precisely that individual sense of self worth. It is just because he possesses such a unique personality that Joseph has been able to rise to the point where he is now able to realize his historical mission and bring his starving people out of a famine-stricken Canaan, guaranteeing, thus, the survival of his race. When on Jacob's death bed, the son admits to his 'crimes', to 'playing fast and loose and for deceit; for childish arrogance and incorrigible naughtiness, [and] for self-esteem and blind conceit', the reader has long before been encouraged to view such misdemeanours as part of the 'comprehensive plan' ('einer weitschauenden Planung') that governs Joseph's life.[169]

Joseph's assumption of a providential role for his actions is warranted by the Biblical source of the story; but it is also Mann's way of bestowing a clear representative value upon his character and his actions. In the midst of Joseph's extended discussion with the Pharoah and his entourage about the source of his clairvoyance, he defines himself as a 'single individual through whom the typical and the traditional are being fulfilled'; and he adds: 'what constitutes civilized life is that the binding and traditional depth shall fulfil itself in the freedom of God which belongs to the I; there is no human civilization without the one and without the other'.[170]

Joseph's insight could well be extended to the very undertaking of *Joseph and his Brothers*: Mann's novel constitutes an epic representation of a coming together of tradition and myth within the life of a remarkable individual. On more than one occasion, the narrator emphasizes that it is only tradition that can give depth to individual identity: 'the deeper the roots of our being go down into the layers that lie below and beyond the fleshly confines of our ego[. . .] the heavier is our life with thought, the weightier is the soul of our flesh', adding on a subsequent occasion: 'for we move in the footsteps of others, and all life is but the pouring of the present into the forms of myth' ('alles Leben ist Ausfüllung mythischer Formen mit Gegenwart').[171] It is Joseph's sense of tradition that gives both substance and form to his journey through life. For, underlying the multitude of sensations, emotions and responses that characterize his experience of the world lies the pattern of anticipation, cyclical change and, above all, repetition. Joseph's progress through life is (as he noted during his second stay in the pit) part of a 'revolving sphere, of the above that becomes below and again mounts upwards, by turns; of the law of opposites, of how order is reversed and things turned upside down', and this formal pattern is reflected in the events of the story.[172] Joseph spends, for example, three days in the first pit and three years in the second, and the seven years he spends in the tutelage of Potiphar exactly mirrors the amount of time his father spent as a 'partner' of his lord, Laban. When Joseph arrives for his audition with the Pharaoh at the city of Blinking, the reader can fully appreciate the feeling of *déjà vu* with which he is overwhelmed: 'it was once more seed-time, time of the burial of the god, as it had been when he came for the second time to the pit and lay in it three days [. . .] Everything fitted in: precisely three years had passed, they were at the same point in the circle, the week of the twenty-second to last day of Choiak, and the children of Egypt had just celebrated once more the feast of the harrowing and the setting-up of the sacred backbone'.[173]

The recurring events and crises in Joseph's story are part of a cyclical structure which lends support to its mythic dimension and timeless relevance. The content of the novel is 'man's spiritual history, the character of his soul', in which Joseph's story occupies the central position. The latter not only provides the medium through which Mann can explore the major themes of providence, redemption and resurrection; it also provides the vehicle for the narrator's extended commentary upon the human condition itself. As the narrator continually makes clear, the events described in the Joseph tetralogy are part of a wider human allegory, in which is manifest the 'connection between the dignity of the self and the dignity of humanity'.[174] This dignity, it is true, is not self-evident or unproblematical; as the narrator observes, the 'door to evil choice' is always open and frequently entered by a human kind that is forever in danger, like Joseph in his most narcissistic mode, of surrendering to the 'dark, deep, silent knowledge of the flesh'.[175] Such temptations are part of the overall picture, and the narrator has much to say on the subject of self-interest, jealousy, suffering, evil and death. Given the historical context in which the Joseph novel series was written, to have forgone a confrontation with the negative aspects of the human personality would have seemed hopelessly Utopian and an evasion of responsibility. Mann's account of the darker side of experience is, nevertheless, balanced by an optimism and a sense of militant humanism that finds expression in the narrator's commentary on hope, love, beauty, piety, faith and forgiveness. These are the values that constitute the *Humanitätsideal* (humanist ideal) which stands at the moral heart of the novel.

This *Humanitätsideal* finds embodiment not only in the figure and exploits of Joseph and his brethren, but also in the values and attitudes evinced by the narrator. It could hardly be otherwise; for *Joseph and His Brothers* is (self-evidently) not the Biblical account of Joseph, but an interpretation and commentary upon that account. If the story itself can be read as a powerful counter myth to the politics of nihilism promulgated from within Nazi Germany, a second counter myth is provided by Mann's narrative treatment of the original and by the values that emerge through the highly personal voice that constantly moves back and forth between the reader and the characters, describing, assessing and interpreting the events of the story. The personal inflection of that narrative voice owes much to the experiences that its author went through while composing his novel in exile. Like Jacob, and Joseph after him, Mann was also a 'refugee from home', and forced to live 'like one who, placed by chance in a certain set of circumstances [. . .] tries to master them as quickly as he may'.[176] The resilience and sense of purpose that Joseph evinces in surviving his ordeals were also shared by Mann who, in spite of losing home, possessions and, eventually, citizenship, succeeded in keeping intact his will to live and to write. The story-teller is, after all, only 'dead and perished' when he or she is cut off from a community of language, 'vanished speechless from that former life without leave or thinkable possibility of breaking silence ('den Bann des Schweigens') without any whatsoever sign';[177] and Mann (like Joseph) was a supreme story-teller, someone whose curiosity and restless energies continually propelled him onwards 'towards fresh adventures which are painstakingly lived through, down to their remotest details, according to the restless spirit's will'.[178]

It is this personal imperative that helps explain the central importance allocated in the novel to the 'art of writing'. It is (Mann insists through the narrator) language which, in organizing history into a narrative, is able to bestow upon the life of an individual and nation alike a degree of consistency and purpose. For history is more than a record of events: it is also the 'stratified record upon which are set our feet, the ground beneath us' ('das Geschichtete und das Geschicht, das unter dem Boden ist').[179] Without the narrative of history, there is no tradition, no 'cosmic procedure', just the 'bottoms and the abysses of the well of the past', out of whose depths the Joseph story ascends.

Tradition must, however, be founded on an adequate and sympathetic understanding of the human condition, otherwise it can grow (as it did in the hands of the Nazis) into a dangerous abstraction. For this reason, 'we all owe it to life and the processes of life ('dem Leben und Fortschritt') to accept and even insist upon the truth', an exhortation that Mann follows in his attempt to give epic shape to Joseph's story in *Joseph and His Brothers*.[180] Mann's concept of 'truth', however, extends well beyond a slavish following of the letter of the Biblical story; not only is the idea of an 'original' version of the story problematic in itself, but the account given in the Old Testament is subject to mild and most respectful criticism, because it lacks, in places, imagination and scope, being a 'drawn and salted and embalmed remnant of the truth, not truth's living lineaments' ('nicht wie ihre Lebensgestalt').[181] The latter can only be produced by a style that is capable of delving into the internal psychological world of the characters whilst keeping in focus the broader external world of history and myth, and it is one of the strengths of *Joseph and His Brothers* that both aspects are handled in such a convincing way by an author capable of registering both the nuances of Joseph's anguish at the bottom of his pit and the epic spectacle that accompanies his entry into the royal cities of Egypt.

There is, however, a second type of truth evident in Mann's novel, one which finds expression not so much in the events and characters themselves, but in a certain attitude that the narrator evinces to these events and characters. Almost as if to counteract the larger than life proportions of the story, the narrator adopts from Joseph's master, Potiphar, a certain 'tolerant irony', a perspective that encourages the reader to accept the values and philosophies espoused by the characters whilst retaining an important distance from them. The reader is never allowed to lose sight of the human weaknesses, foibles and occasional absurdities that also characterize Joseph's story. If we should smile, for example, with the narrator as he describes how Joseph's ancestors, seeking an omen for their actions, attempt to read the future from the entrails of a pigeon, it is a smile of sympathy rather than of malice. It is this gently ironic point of view that allows Mann to reach into the moral heart of the Biblical story without succumbing to the irrational mystique that (as he would have realized watching his contemporary

Germany) attends such attempts to make the past relevant to the present.

Mann completed the final volume of the Joseph novel, *Joseph the Provider*, in January 1943. The previous year had been a dark year both for Thomas Mann and the democratic world in general, for Hitler and his rapacious war machine had shown themselves to be virtually unstoppable in its rapid subjugation of a demoralized Europe. In his many radio speeches to Europe made at this time, Mann did all he could to warn his country-men and others of the catastrophe that would lie ahead should Hitler be victorious. Now, more than ever, the case for a militant humanism needed to be made, for a worldview capable of marrying the values of reason, good faith and enlightenment to the exigencies of power. This moral imperative is also evident in the final sections of the Joseph novel, which does not end, as the Biblical account does, with Joseph's death, but with the hero very much alive and speculating upon the uses and abuses of power. Here, in the final pages, we learn that the latter is not a force evil in itself; Joseph's rise to wealth and prestige in Egypt was, after all, entirely due to the many gifts, intellectual, social and linguistic with which nature had provided him. These gifts were the basis of Joseph's power over others, which had at first negative and then positive consequences. Without power nothing can be achieved, but to employ it for its own sake is a dangerous and 'absurd' folly. Its exercise must be tempered by the same kind of capacity to forgive that Joseph now shows, as his final action in the story, towards his wayward brothers. If that can happen, we may still have the chance of escaping from what the narrator earlier had eloquently, but most ominously, termed the 'moral terrors of the underworld'.[182]

# 8

# Thomas Mann and the Germans: *Doctor Faustus*

In June 1944, five years into his period of exile in America, Thomas Mann became a citizen of his adopted country. The decision had not been taken lightly; even in the darkest moments of its history, Mann had always thought of himself as a specifically German writer, as part of a cultural and linguistic tradition that reached back well beyond the medieval period. His decision to become an American citizen required, then, a good deal of emotional and psychological preparation; but it also gave Mann the opportunity to speculate upon his 'German' identity and upon the whole notion of 'Germanness'. Indeed, within a month of the conferment of his citizenship, Mann became embroiled in an exchange with the noted modern linguist and Professor of French at Yale University, Henri Peyre, about precisely this issue. Peyre had divined in one of Mann's essays, 'What is German?', a plea for a 'soft peace' for Germany once the war had been settled. Mann, not without a little pain and embarrassment, attempted to refute the accusation in a later article, 'My Defence', arguing that the sole aim of his earlier pronouncements had been to 'identify, objectively and psychologically, certain traits of German character with which I am only too familiar and which have become disastrous for Germany and the world'.[183]

To further his 'defence' against Peyre, Mann might well have pointed to the publications that he had already produced as part of this extensive investigation into Germany, the German character and National Socialism. Even Mann's apparently apolitical fiction of this period, such as the novel, *Lotte in Weimar*, published in 1939, bears traces of this growing concern to identify the specifically German sources of political irrationality and illiberality. The novel describes the reunion after 44 years of Goethe with his childhood sweetheart, Charlotte Buff, who had provided the model for the heroine of his famous epistolary novel: *The Sorrows of Young Werther* (1774). Mann's reconstruction of this imaginary reunion remains largely within the personal mode, but carefully avoids the dangers of sentimentality in its description of the coming together of the two lovers *manqués*. The novel also deals with the more philosophical theme of the complexity (and even inaccessibility) of personality, as the narrative gradually pieces together out of the conversations, judgements and aperçues provided by a number of Goethe's friends (and would-be friends) an image of the contradictory personality of the aged artist, in one place making a rare, but highly successful, use of the interior monologue or *erlebte Rede* technique, in an attempt to get even closer to the psychology of his character.

*Lotte in Weimar* is a distinctly personal novel; but it also looks 'outwards' to the wider world beyond the somewhat oppressive society of nineteenth-century Weimar that forms the context of the story, to engage with notions of 'the German' and 'Germanness'. On more than one occasion, Mann uses Goethe as a persona to voice his own mistrust of the German people, who 'abandon themselves credulously to every fanatic scoundrel who speaks to their baser qualities, confirms them in their vices, teaches them nationality means barbarism and isolation'.[184] When the aged poet exclaims in the midst of his interior monologue that he can accept the noble in the German soul but 'not this pig-headed craving to be a unique nation, this national narcissism that wants to make its own stupidity a pattern and a power over the rest of the world' he is expressing an opinion that Mann later will voice in his own analysis of the surrender of contemporary Germany to the politics of violence and unreason.[185]

Although *Lotte in Weimar* provides in its margins an early indication of Mann's desire to confront the specifically German roots of National Socialism, it was certainly not conceived as a vehicle for an extended exploration of this issue. Mann postponed such a treatment until 1945, when he published the essay 'Deutchland und die Deutschen' ('Germany and the Germans'). Building upon Mann's earlier discussion of the subject in 'What is German?', the essay attempts a highly condensed intellectual history of what Mann terms the 'complex world of German psychology'.[186] The combination of apparently contradictory features that Mann notes in the German character, such as its cosmopolitanism and provincialism, its hankering for recognition from the rest of the world (that is combined with an excessive absorption in local tradition and custom) and its world-famous philosophy and contributions to modern technology (that exist alongside its fanaticism and unpredictable self-surrender to political passion) are traits that he discovers in Germany's major intellectual and cultural figures from Luther to Nietzsche. The Germans (Mann argues) have never known how to reconcile the individual and the social, preferring to define freedom as either a hopelessly inward-looking dimension of the private self or as the military superiority of their nation over others. Cut off from, and dismissive of, the rest of the world, the Germans have been drawn throughout their history to political, religious and military solutions that transcend and negate many of the humanist assumptions that underscore Western civilization. Looking for one representative of German culture who embodies the many traits of this trans-historical image of the German character, Mann invokes the legendary medieval figure of Faust, the 'lonely thinker and inquirer, theologian and philosopher' whose longing for worldly pleasure and conquest led to his infamous pact with the devil. The rise to power of Hitler in Germany has, Mann concludes, provided a context in which the legend of Faust has gained a new relevance, making it the perfect metaphor for the crimes of a nation that is 'quite literally, going to hell'.[187]

Mann's major novel of this period, *Doctor Faustus*, begun in 1943 and published in 1947, turns this suggestive metaphor into an epic work of literature. *Doctor Faustus* is written in the form of a biography of a musician who, in seeking an ever increasing refinement and sophistication of artistic expression, surrenders his soul to the devil in return for a guarantee that he will achieve his goals. In making his Faustian hero an artist, Mann returns to the milieu that so fascinated him in the early years of his career, and Leverkühn embodies many of the traits of these early artist figures: Tonio Kröger's single-minded dedication to his art; Gustav von Aschenbach's facility for aesthetic speculation in *Death in Venice*; and the aloofness from the 'bourgeois' society that is the hallmark of Detlev Spinell, the protagonist of the early short story, 'Tristan'. Adrian Leverkühn is, however, not simply an artist; he is also a *German* one (a point that is reinforced in the sub-title of the novel). For this reason it is highly significant that, unlike all of Mann's previous artist figures, the hero of *Doctor Faustus* is not a writer but a musician. For, as Mann had pointed out in 'Germany and the Germans', music is the cultural form that most closely corresponds to the 'abstract' and 'mythical' bent of the German character, providing a medium through which the German penchant for 'inwardness' and the 'daemonic', (those elements of the German character that Mann believed had contributed to the neurosis of National Socialism) could best find expression.[188]

From the very beginning of his novel, Mann emphasizes the presence of the daemonic and the illicit at the heart of Leverkühn's ancestral background. Adrian's father, Jonathan Leverkühn, a small farmer of Saxon origins, may be 'of the best German type', and happy in his marriage to a wife endowed with 'native, instinctive taste'; but it is also the case that he is an intellectually restless figure, whose horizons extend well beyond the modest homestead into which Adrian Leverkühn is born. For alongside his Lutheran piety, Leverkühn's father possesses a penchant for investigating the 'mysteries of nature', including exotic specimen of lepidoptera, insects and butterflies.[189] Such creatures occupy a highly ambiguous position between artifice and nature, being able to mutate their pigmentation and adopt a variety of appearances. These strange and ambiguous creatures often, like the butterfly *Hetaera esmeralda*, possess a barely perceptible imperfection on their surface, which hints at the toxic reality that lies beneath their fateful beauty. The world that so attracts father Leverkühn belongs, in short, to that of the paranormal, where 'poison and beauty, poison and magic, even magic and ritual' reign.[190] As such, Adrian's father is transgressing the limits of acceptable scientific knowledge in a way reminiscent of that other practitioner of the black arts, Johannes Faust.

The presence of the irrational and mystical in Adrian's life is further enhanced by his move to boarding school in the neighbouring town of Kaisersachern. Although this part of the story takes place in the outgoing years of the nineteenth century, Kaisersachern has retained much of the 'old-world, underground neurosis' of the medieval period, a period characterized by forces of irrationality that often took the shape of 'fantastic

and mystical folk-movements'. Kaisersachern embodies the
more sinister side of the penchant for the arcane and mystical
evident in the idiosyncratic predilections of Leverkühn's father.
Not mystery but violence and excess hang in the air, as does a
certain unhealthy ethical and political hankering after 'the Folk'
('das Volk').[191] If transgression assumed an intellectual form in
Leverkühn the elder, within the morbid shadow world of Kaisersachern it points ominously to the 'deeds of sinister significance'
that will take place in the not too distant future of German
history.

It is within this context that Adrian Leverkühn first discovers
his inclination towards music, and it is significant that, even at
this early stage, he finds himself instinctively groping for a form
of expression beyond conventional musical language. Leverkühn
is encouraged in his early experiments by his music teacher,
Wendell Kretzschmar, whose highly involved reading of the late
Beethoven inspires the young Leverkühn to define his own
musical aesthetic. Kretzschmar elevates Beethoven into a Faustian hero of the mind, a lonely artist whose daring journey into
previously uncharted areas of musical expression put him at
odds with an incredulous society. In Beethoven's late piano
sonatas, Kretzschmar argues, the composer was able to unite
subjective expression with objective convention in a way un-
paralleled in musical history. In sacrificing his health and life for
such a venture, Beethoven pointed the way to yet a further stage
in musical evolution, wherein the 'merely personal [. . .] once
more outgrew itself, in that it entered into the mythical, the
collectively great and supernatural'.[192] The composer who eventually took this road was Richard Wagner, whose 'cosmogonic
myth of the *Ring*' best makes use of the 'elemental, the primitive
and the primeval' musical values espoused by Kretzschmar in a
later lecture. It is, however, the eighteenth-century Pennsyl-
vanian German, Johann Conrad Beissel, who exerts the initial
influence upon Leverkühn. He is, admittedly, an obscure figure,
an amateur composer and charismatic preacher, whom Zeitblom (Leverkühn's *confidant* and the narrator of the novel)
pointedly dismisses as a 'backwoods dictator'. Beissel's importance for Leverkühn lies in the fact that he succeeded in control-
ling the sentimentality inherent in his inspirational religious
hymns by imposing a 'sense of order' upon his compositions.[193]
His compositions represent the victory of musical form over

sound and, as such, they point the way towards the highly self-conscious music that Leverkühn himself will eventually produce.

Wagner and Beissel represent the two musical models upon which Leverkühn will develop his own aesthetic: the elemental and the formally chaste. Leverkühn takes his first steps in this direction under the tutorship of Kretzschmar. It is whilst a student of the latter that Leverkühn first learns that not only has music lost its original religious significance, it is no longer even regarded as a medium that has anything new to offer the creative artist. What capacity it had for giving expression to the inward world of the emotions was exhausted by the great Romantic composers of the nineteenth century, particularly Beethoven and Wagner. Deprived of its outward-looking social function, and exhausted in its ability to explore the purely subjective realm, the 'methods and conventions' of modern music (indeed, of all modern art) seem to Leverkühn 'good for parody only'.[194]

This insight encourages Leverkühn to look back on musical tradition with (as the wary Zeitblom notes) a 'combination of scepticism [and] intellectual reserve' ('geistige Schamhaftigkeit'), as he explores one well-trodden genre after another, from the *Lied* to the *opéra bouffe*.[195] He has reached a point similar to his Faustian namesake where a movement into the future and a new musical language is only possible through a radical break with the past and its traditions, even if that means committing moral transgression. Like the tragic figure of Beethoven in Kretschmar's musical pantheon, to achieve his 'breakthrough', Leverkühn must also 'die' to the world, renouncing, for the sake of his art, the normal and the healthy. This he achieves by consciously contracting syphilis from a lady of the night, Esmeralda. Like those strange creatures studied by father Leverkühn, Esmeralda also combines physical beauty with an inner reality that is diseased; in possessing her, the young composer gives (to a shocked Zeitblom) the first sign of a 'mysterious longing for daemonic conception'.[196] Leverkühn's relationship with Esmeralda symbolizes his departure from the world, for the disease, evoking as it does a similar event in the life of the German philosopher, Friedrich Nietzsche (whose Faustian inclinations paralleled Leverkühn's own) will eventually lead to madness and death.

'Liberated' through disease from the claims of the bourgeois world, Leverkühn begins to lay the basis for a new musical system, which will have nothing in common with the humanist traditions of musical culture within which he has been forced to work, even in a parodistic fashion. What he arrives at is a method of 'strict composition' ('strengen Satz'), a system of twelve semitones 'from which a piece and all the movements of a work must strictly derive'.[197] Leverkühn's new method bears remarkable similarities to the form of musical notation developed by Arnold Schoenberg and other members of the Viennese School of Music that flourished in the early part of this century, and Mann was compelled to include a postscript acknowledging his debt to the famous Austrian composer. The debt is, however, a purely formal one, for Leverkühn's new music connotes a series of political values that Schoenberg would have totally rejected. Leverkühn wishes to substitute the harmonic freedoms of nineteenth-century music with a 'self-imposed compulsion to order' that leaves nothing to chance and little to individual creativity and, as such, prefigures the political direction towards fascism that his country is about to take.

The first compositions, however, that emerge out of this new system give little indication of being of epoch-making significance; they are minor pieces, 'self-centred and completely cool esoteric', which appeal merely to the connoisseur.[198] It is a music that satisfies the first premise of Leverkühn's initial aesthetic, a purity of form, but falls well short of achieving the second premise: the desire to re-establish modern music on an elemental or mythic footing. To achieve the latter, a second act of transgression must be undertaken by the Faustian hero, one that will lead not to the loss of health but to the loss of soul.

It is Faust's pact with the devil that constitutes the central scene of the original legend, forming the pivotal moment in which the medieval over-reacher's commitment to the forces of darkness becomes irrevocable. In Goethe's classic version, the *Urfaust*, Mephistopheles presents himself to the bewildered Faust as a 'part of darkness, mother of the light';[199] Leverkühn's spirit of the underworld, however, is not a 'a prince of darkness', but a bully and rogue, suitably garbed in the livery of the street vendor and charlatan. For what Leverkühn's satanic tempter offers *his* Faust is not knowledge but (in a sense) anti-knowledge, the incentive to disregard the values of humanist culture, and the courage to 'dare to be barbaric, twice barbaric indeed, because of coming after the humane, after all possible root-treatment and bourgeois *raffinement*. After the pact, Leverkühn will be able finally to dispense with what this satanic tempter and his new vassal both agree are the outmoded musical values of the 'bourgeois age', replacing them with a music that can give expression to 'excess, paradox, the mystic passion, the utterly unbourgeois ordeal'.[200]

What Leverkühn has committed himself to are the values of a virulent anti-humanism, and this soon becomes evident in the music that he composes after his pact with the devil. In works such as the *Symphonia Cosmologica*, the gently ironic tone of his earlier compositions is now heightened into what the shocked Zeitblom describes as a 'nihilistic sacrilege'.[201] Leverkühn's latest musical compositions, such as the aptly named *Apocalipsis cum figuris*, have much in common with those other forms of 'reactionary modernism' that came to prominence in the post-war period in Germany after 1918. This was a period that witnessed many attacks upon the political ideas of 'bourgeois' liberalism. In the novel, this trend is represented by the Krid-wiss circle, a group of intellectuals and academics who espouse a 'many-sided, yes, all-embracing critique of the bourgeois tradi-tion', of that system of political and moral life that was founded upon the 'values of culture, enlightenment, [and] humanity'.[202] The Kridwiss circle argue that this system must be dismantled, by force, if necessary, and replaced by the 'far higher court of violence, authority, [and] the dictatorship of belief'.[203] Lever-kühn is not formally a part of this circle, but (as Zeitblom notes) his music embodies many of the traits of the irrationality and illiberalism preached by this group of right-wing thinkers.

Leverkühn's affinities with the Kridwiss circle not only clarify the larger moral and political implications of his musical direc-tion; they also establish the contemporary historical relevance of this direction, revealing it as something more than just the folly of an individual artist following a highly idiosyncratic path towards madness and infamy. At one point in the story, at the critical juncture where Leverkühn is on the brink of giving up his theological studies to devote himself to music, Wendall Kretz-schmar voices the following generalization: 'Art strides on, [. . .] and does so through the medium of the personality, which is the product and the tool of the time, and in which objective and subjective motives combine indistinguishably, each taking on the shape of the others'.[204] Kretzschmar might well have been

speaking for Mann himself here, who conceived of his novel as
the 'novel of my era, disguised as the story of an artist's life, a
terribly imperiled and sinful artist'.[205] *Doctor Faustus* was intended, then, as a political allegory on the condition of Mann's
contemporary Germany, a concern that is reflected in the
attention to time and historical detail evident in the novel. Not
only are we able to date quite precisely the development of
Leverkühn's musical career (from 1885 to 1930), but even
Zeitblom's narration of the life of his friend has its own time-
scale (from 1943 to 1945). The effect of the interweaving of these
two time-scales is to make quite explicit the historical implications of Leverkühn's personal tragedy.

*Doctor Faustus* is not, however, a historical novel in the conventional sense of the term. It does not attempt to describe the
major political, social or diplomatic changes that took place
during the period covered by the novel. Nor, although its origins
lay in Mann's desire to make sense of the rise of National
Socialism in Germany, does it focus on Hitler or The Third
Reich. Unlike the work of a number of other exiled writers,
including that of his own son Klaus (who published his novel of
anti-fascism, *Mephisto*, in 1936), Mann does not attempt to
depict the phenomenon of National Socialism in any *direct* way:
none of the Nazi hierarchy appear in the novel, and the reader
will look in vain for any sign of storm-troopers, street fighting,
marches, political rallies or any of the other activities that
accompanied the Nazi seizure of power. Even anti-semitism
plays but a marginal role in Leverkühn's story.

In the place of a literal representation of events, Mann draws
our attention to the intellectual myths that have influenced the
course of recent German history. He was, for example, fully
aware of the role played by the First World War in bringing an
end to the *ancien régime* of Wilhelmine Germany and in preparing the way for a new era of mass politics. But the pages that
describe that military engagement return the reader to the
central legend that underscored and helped legitimate that
offensive: the Faust myth. What Germany hoped to achieve in
1914 was no less than a 'breakthrough' to a greater status in the
world. Zeitblom later captures the presumption that lay behind
this Faustian ambition: 'we would become a dominating world
power – but such a position is not to be achieved by means of
mere moral "home-work". War, then, and if needs must, war

against everybody, to convince everybody and to win; that was our lot, our "sending".[206]

Both Leverkühn's overweening musical ambition and the reckless expansionist strategy of the German military machine have, then, the same intellectual source, a 'tragically mythical' attachment to the 'psychology of the breakthrough'.[207] For that reason, the link the novel forges between the German history of this period and Leverkühn's music is largely an intellectual and symbolic one. To be sure, in many places in the novel Mann departs from the main plot to offer a highly perceptive insight into the social mores of pre-war Munich, the political turmoil of the November 'Revolution', and the fragile world of the Weimar Republic. In these episodes, Mann adds an important social dimension to the novel, which complements his descriptions of the highly intense world of Leverkühn's music. We are introduced in such passages to a range of minor characters, from the charming Anglophile and minor poet, Rüdiger Schildknapp, through to a series of more tragic characters, such as the Rodde sisters, whose complicated personal lives give a glimpse into the decadence and moral decline that exists 'under cover of the bourgeois propriety' of this post-war period.[208] The suicide of Clarissa Rodde and the murder of her sister's paramour by the latter's outraged husband, Helmut Institoris, seem to be in keeping with a period in German history in which individual standards and good sense gave way to the 'horrible, senseless [and] irrational'.[209] These intimate sub-plots do much to reinforce the daemonic restlessness and amoral import of Adrian Leverkühn and the music he composes.

The affinity between Leverkühn's music and the ideological direction of his age is established by yet a further set of characters. These range from the two theological *Dozenten* under whom Leverkühn studies as an undergraduate in Halle, Ehrenfried Kumpf and Eberward Schleppfuss, through to his youthful and idealistic *Wandervögel* companions, and includes the Kridwiss circle itself, whose views are anticipated by that lone spokesman for the irrational, Chaim Breisacher. What this diverse group has in common is an adherence to the philosophy of the Conservative Revolution, a political and intellectual movement that hoped to bring about the abolition of the nineteenth-century liberal system of government and its replacement by a more uniquely German system, based on the spirit of self-sacrifice, respect for tradition and obedience to authority.[210]

Explicit politics, it is true, is very far from the minds of Kumpf and Schleppfuss; but the former's penchant for diabolic speculations in 'good plain German' and the latter's more ominous delving into the 'daemonic conception of God and the universe' exert a lasting influence upon the impressionable Leverkühn.[211] The metaphysical speculations that Kumpf and Schleppfuss enter into are obscure in the extreme, and they themselves as characters have something comical about them, an element of the archaic and bizarre that Mann attempts to connote even in their names. This is not the case with Leverkühn's association with the *Wandervögel*. These are not eccentric theologians but representatives of the well-bred, middle-class youth of pre-war Germany. As harbingers of the 'new' Germany, their pronouncements are given greater space and weight by Leverkühn and the narrator alike. Like all *Wandervögel* groups, this collection of like-minded youths devotes itself to an enjoyment of 'music, nature and joyous worship' within a natural setting reached after hiking through countryside. But once at their destination, tents pitched and their community formed, this vehemently nationalist cohort (led by the aptly named Teutleben and Deutschlin ('Teutonic-living' and 'Little-German') give themselves over to speculations on how Germany can best counter the 'decline in faith' ('Zerfall') and 'disintegration' that are the hallmarks of the new age.[212] The solutions that they arrive at hark back to the Faustian motif that runs through the novel and anticipate Leverkühn's musical development. Out of their overbearing sense of youth (a feature that all agree is uniquely German), they will draw the strength to 'stand up and shake off the fetters of an outlived civilization, to dare – where others lack courage – to plunge again into the elemental', and in doing so vouchsafe the world 'some renewal, some revolution', which will make full use of the 'daemonic powers' that attend any vital political movement. Forced to descend from the heights of idealist speculation to consider the practical dimension of such a revolution, they conclude by identifying the two remaining avenues that are open for the future: the 'two possibilities of religious submission and religious realization: the social and the national'.[213]

The radically Utopian ideas that the *Wandervögel* espouse mirror the psychology of breakthrough that is a central part of

Leverkühn's musical aesthetic. But their 'philosophy' is as romantic as it is critical and, whilst the language that they employ to promulgate their vision of the future is close to the rhetoric of National Socialism, their enthusiasm for the future has its roots in idealism rather than the power-centred pragmatism that will follow it.

This is not the case with the subsequent exponents of the Conservative Revolution that Leverkühn (and his amanuenses, Zeitblom) encounter: Chaim Breisacher and the members of the Kridwiss circle. The version of the Conservative Revolution that Breisacher expounds contains none of the idealism and enthusiasm of the *Wandervögel*, but consists of an arrogant and sneering dismissal of all aspects of Western culture from the Bible to modern music. It is a 'radical conservatism' devoid of ideals save one: a deification of the 'genuine folk', whose rituals are coming to form a new religion that will make considerations of morality irrelevant and antiquated. As Zeitblom observes, Breisacher's 'crass and malicious conservatism' has nothing in common with the values that have been traditionally associated with conservatism: a respect for tradition and established institutions, a wish to preserve the past and a suspicion of radical change (represented in this particular episode by the Baron von Riedesel).[214] Not construction but destruction, not stability but disorder, not consensus but confrontation are the goals of this new revolutionary conservatism.

It is this fact which explains the respect which is accorded to force and violence in this philosophy. As the life of the Weimar Republic accelerates towards its end, revolutionary conservatism swiftly turns into an apocalyptic worldview, into a welcoming of the 'liberating' sensation of catastrophe. This feeling is particularly widespread in the Kridwiss circle. Taking their cue from Georges Sorel's significantly titled *Reflexions on Violence*, this group of scholars, writers and art critics welcomes the 'mounting barbarism' that they see around them on the politically strife-torn streets of German cities. Crisis, they hope, will prepare the way for a new society based upon force and the tyranny of the masses instead of upon reason and respect for the individual. The future will be harsh, 'an age of over-all wars and revolutions', in which only the fittest will survive, even if this should require the 'large-scale elimination of the unfit, the diseased and the weak-minded'.[215]

The members of the Kridwiss circle come close to expounding
the ideologies and policies of fascism proper, and it is apt that
Zeitblom's exposure to their ideas should, at this point in the
story, prompt him into a re-evaluation of the political and moral
implications of his hero's musical aesthetic. What worries the
loyal Zeitblom about his companion's latest composition, the
*Apocalypse*, is precisely its affinities with the rejection of humanism found in the Kridwiss circle. Certainly, the increasingly
single-minded composer is capable of producing the 'purest
music', but such purity is only achieved by recourse to the
musical techniques of the pre-cultural era, a 'stage of civilisation
not only priestly but primitive'. Leverkühn's music represents
'calculation raised to mystery' and, in spite of his loyal defence of
the work, Zeitblom cannot help but register his misgivings: it
demonstrates 'how near aestheticism and barbarism are to each
other'.[216]

It is fitting that it is through Zeitblom that the historical and
political relevance of Leverkühn's art should receive its fullest
discussion. For it is his narrative that brings together the two
dimensions of the novel: the local, personal world of Leverkühn's
artistic career and the larger, historical development of Germany
in the first half of this century. Zeitblom is able to perform this
mediating role because, as friend and confidant of the hero from
childhood onwards, he is both part of Leverkühn's fate but also,
as its retrospective chronicler, separate from it. It is in this latter
capacity, as Leverkühn's biographer, that Zeitblom's importance largely lies. This is not to argue that he is, in the main part
of the story, without depth or interest; but he remains a secondary character, a vicarious observer of the recurrent artistic crises
experienced by his hero, and without the power to influence the
latter's course as a musician. To a large extent, this secondary
role is self-chosen, for Zeitblom holds fast to what even he
describes as the highly romantic separation of 'the artist and
the ordinary man' ('Gegensatz von Künstlertum und Bürger-
lichkeit').[217] In their many conversations Zeitblom plays the foil
to Leverkühn's often iconoclastic views on modern music and its
relationship to tradition and, even when he cannot accept the
direction that his friend's musical development is taking, he
often chooses to smother his criticisms, remaining by Leverkühn's side vexed and in silent reflection. Even at the height of
his greatest reservations regarding Leverkühn's music, Zeitblom

finds his emotions in a confused state. He responds, for example, to his first encounter with the music of the *Apocalypse* with a mixture of emotions, 'horror, amazement, consternation and pride', that leaves him trembling and in emotional disarray.[218] When he is in the immediate vicinity of his hero, Zeitblom can do little more than register a combination of conflicting responses, remaining torn between his fascination for and love of Leverkühn's aloof and mysterious personality, on the one hand, and his disquiet over the moral implications of the same personality, on the other.

It is only after Leverkühn's death that the spirit of the Faustian hero can be exorcised and Zeitblom can himself assume a quasi artistic role as the author of Leverkühn's 'biography'. It is significant that the novel begins, in fact, three years after Leverkühn's death in 1940, with a self-portrayal of the narrator. The very first description of Zeitblom establishes him as a character who stands for all the personal qualities that his hero and the various exponents of the Conservative Revolution negate, being a person 'wholly moderate of temper [. . .] both healthy and humane, addressed to reason and harmony'.[219] Zeitblom is alone in the novel in the possession of such qualities and, although he finds cause to make light of himself and the 'ethical narrow-mindedness' that arises from the classic-humanist culture that he espouses (and practises as a school-teacher in Bavaria), it is precisely the exercise of such qualities that allows him to make the necessary connections between Leverkühn's music and the contemporary state of Germany.

Zeitblom's point of view is characterized by a dual perspective that allows him 'to point out both the personal and the objective, the time in which the narrator moves and that in which the narrative does'.[220] At one point in his narrative he halts the story to emphasize how 'the excited state bound up with my subject constantly assimilates itself to that produced by the shattering events of the time'.[221] Indeed, Zeitblom moves backwards and forwards between the two time spheres, using the immediate context of his narration (the period between 1943 and 1945) as a way of assessing and commenting upon the events that take place during the story-time of the novel (which covers the years between 1905 and 1930). As the novel progresses, the parallels between the two spheres become increasingly clearer until the point is reached where they converge in the shape of Leverkühn's final composition, the *Lamentation of Doctor Faustus*, which seems a perfect expression of the horror and tragedy that emerges during the final days of Nazi Germany.

Zeitblom's own understanding of the historical course of his contemporary Germany develops and deepens as the narrative unfolds. He begins the story as someone who, although critical of the stance of the 'Führer' on issues such as the 'Jewish question', is nevertheless sufficiently patriotic to feel a thrill of pride on hearing the news of the success of German U-boats in the North Atlantic.[222] At this stage in the novel, Zeitblom's attitude to Germany corresponds to the benign position that he adopts towards the subject of his 'biography': Adrian Leverkühn. Changes in his response to the latter accompany and, to a large extent, are produced by Zeitblom's increasing revulsion about the course of the war and the atrocities perpetrated by the Nazi regime. As the 'sheer horror' of the Nazi crimes becomes more evident, Zeitblom, the apolitical humanist and custodian of classical culture, gradually comes to adopt a more political perspective on events, at one point even expressing a preference for the mass politics of Communism over that represented by the Nazi regime.[223] He also assumes a more critical perspective towards himself. When the gates of the extermination camps are finally opened to reveal a spectacle of unimaginable horror within, the citizens of Germany are forced to confront the 'torture chamber' that resided at the heart of their nation for several long years. Zeitblom's final message, however, is that the burden of guilt should be shared by all; not only by those, like Leverkühn, who made the Faustian gamble, but also by others, such as himself, who were held in awe by the spectacle. And as the worthy *Bürger* of Weimar file past the charred remains of Nazi victims, Zeitblom exhorts them to confront the abominations before them: 'Let them look, I look with them. In spirit I let myself be shouldered into their dazed or shuddering ranks'.[224]

Germany must now reap the consequences of its own pact with the devil. In order to attain global self-aggrandizement, a nation was prepared to countenance a regime that mocked and finally annihilated not only personal freedom but the lives of millions of innocent people. Leverkühn's fatherland is now condemned (as Zeitblom sees it) to a fate that will banish it from the civilized world, leaving it 'standing wild-eyed in face of the void'.[225] We might expect Germany's fate to be mirrored by

Leverkühn's own, since he too has entered into a similar unholy pact. His final composition, *The Lamentation of Doctor Faustus*, conceived as a work that will 'take back' the humanity and optimism of Beethoven's Ninth Symphony, does, indeed, seem to confirm this fateful affinity. This 'dark tone-poem' moves in a realm of 'hellish yelling', of a cacophony of sound that culminates in the descent of Faust into the underworld. Goethe ended his classic version of the legend with his hero surrounded by a choir of heavenly hosts, but Leverkühn's composition leaves its composer, to the very end, bereft of 'consolation, appeasement, [or] transfiguration'. In *The Lamentation of Doctor Faustus*, 'final despair achieves a voice' as Leverkühn brings himself to the brink of the 'blackness of his spirit's night' that will overwhelm him in his final years of madness.[226]

One of the first major studies to appear on the novel after its publication in 1947 concluded that *Doctor Faustus* leaves the reader grimly trapped within a 'world without transcendence' and within a vision supported purely by a 'politics of resentment'.[227] There is, certainly, no denying that the novel constitutes a moral condemnation of the arrogant and nihilistic mentality that had encouraged Mann's homeland to enter into a pact with the devil by embracing National Socialism. It could hardly have been otherwise. Mann had been a principled antagonist of Nazism since it first appeared in the late 1920s and had attempted once before, in his short story of 1930, *Mario and the Magician*, to analyse the psychological techniques used by that political movement to win popular support. *Doctor Faustus*, goes well beyond the parameters of that story by showing how fascist ideas and values had permeated large sections of German society (incuding its most educated strata) well before the advent of Hitler. From Leverkühn's theological mentors through to the youthful *Wandervögel* and the members of the Kridwiss circle, the novel is criss-crossed by characters held in sway by the philosophy of irrationalism and intoxicated by the redemptive promise of violence and chaos. With the sole exception of the kindly but ultimately ineffectual Zeitblom, Mann's novel does not contain a sole character capable of resisting the nihilism that ultimately underscores the Conservative Revolution in Germany.

And yet this is not a world entirely bereft of light. At that very moment in which the Faust legend reaches its climax, Mann

breaks with its grim inevitability to point to the faintest suggestion of hope beyond the all-embracing despair. In doing so, he
renounces, for once, the ironic perspective that he had made his
own. In earlier works, such as *The Magic Mountain*, irony had
served to deflate ideals where they might have been expected to
flourish. Now paradox will reverse that process, and affirm
ideals where they cannot hope to exist: in the mind of the
deranged Faustian and in the heart of a dejected nation. As
Zeitblom watches his friend mentally and physically deteriorate
in the process of his *dementia*, he notices that the latter has
acquired an 'Ecco-homo countenance', the visage of Christ-like
suffering.[228] This glimpse of spirituality is evident also in
Leverkühn's final composition. *The Lamentation*, Zeitblom implies, is not a celebration of evil but a lament for the suffering evil
entails and, as such, contains a premonition of the 'mystic idea of
salvation'. After the satanic fury of Leverkühn's piece has taken
its course, a new note is heard on the 'cello, a faint 'whisper', but
in a key that Zeitblom interprets as indicating a 'hope beyond
hopelessness, the transcendence of despair' as it emerges, out of
the moral turpitude that surrounds Leverkühn, Zeitblom and
reader alike, to abide 'as a light in the night'.[229]

# 9

# The Play of Eroticism: *The Confessions of Felix Krull*

In a letter written to his daughter Erika a year before his death in 1955, Thomas Mann wondered whether the works that had occupied him so fully during the last years of his life were not somewhat superfluous, an 'overhanging epilogue' to the literature that had preceded them. He added: 'Often I can't help thinking that it would have been better if I had departed from this earth after *Faustus*. That, after all, was a book of seriousness and [of] a certain power, and would have been a neat finale to a life's labour'.[230] It is understandable why Mann should have thought in this fashion. *Doctor Faustus* can indeed be read as Mann's final statement on a number of issues that had preoccupied him throughout his career as a writer: the amoral nature of the artist and artistic creation; the risk to physical and mental health that knowledge and the quest for greater knowledge brings; the German devotion to music as a source of transcendence; the affinities that this art form has with death; and the dangers of the application of mystical and irrational ideas to the social and political sphere. These themes and others are confronted in *Doctor Faustus*, and within a historical context that leaves the reader in no doubt about the moral import of that novel or about its relevance to the fate of the German nation.

The only major novel to follow that epic narrative, *The Confessions of Felix Krull: Confidence Man* constitutes a departure from the high seriousness evident in *Doctor Faustus* and in much of Mann's earlier fiction. The dark world of moral and intellectual transgression in which Adrian Leverkühn and many of Mann's other characters moved is here abandoned, as is much of the metaphysical complexity that successive generations of readers have found so challenging in the great novels of Mann's corpus, from *The Magic Mountain* to *Doctor Faustus*. But much is gained by this new direction, notably a sense of playfulness and lightness of tone that makes *Felix Krull* one of the more accessible and cosmopolitan of Mann's novels. With this final work, we move into a brighter and less problematic social world, governed not by artistic introspection and guilt but by energy, charm and a highly playful quest for money, prestige and sex. In *Felix Krull*, Mann makes contact with the great tradition of European novel writing, from Defoe to Balzac, in which society had always been seen as a natural milieu. As Mann noted in a letter written in 1953 (shortly after he had resumed work on the uncompleted novel) Balzac's novels, in particular, communicate a sense of energy and spectacle, and a sheer *joie de vivre* that is irresistible, encouraging the reader to devour them, one after the other: 'For they are actually made for devouring: suspenseful, sensational, powerfully told, often unbearably romantic, though almost always talking about money, sentimental, even hypo-critical, but with an enormous sense of the social, at the same time with adventurous sympathy for criminal revolt *against* society. In general they are of a wild grandeur which seems to me always to spring out of the pages.'[231]

The energy and exuberance that Mann admired in Balzac is fully evident in *The Confessions of Felix Krull*. Mann began the novel in 1910, publishing extracts in 1911 and 1922, before completing the final version in 1955.[232] He was later to outline the source of his inspiration in the following way: 'What intrigued me stylistically was the directness of the auto-biographical form, which I had never before tried [...]. At the same time, a peculiar intellectual attraction emanated from the burlesque idea of taking a much-loved tradition – self portraiture in the Goethe manner, the introspective confessions of the born aristocrat – and transferring it to the criminal sphere'.[233] As a model, Mann turned to the genre of the picaresque novel, which had for centuries dealt with the often risqué exploits of its hero in a frank and amusing way. On one level his novel can be read as a straightforward example of that genre, as a record of the 'immediate experience, errors and passions' of the highly gifted and self-promoting confidence trickster, Felix Krull.[234] As is typical of that genre, the story is related in the first person by Krull himself who, looking back over the early period of his life, tells how he was able to rise from near destitution to a position of aristocratic privilege through his innate ability as a confidence man. Krull is both the most cosmopolitan and the most sociable of Mann's heroes. Throughout his highly peripatetic career, he practises his 'silent game of exchanging roles' in a number of locations, initially in his native Rhineland, then in Frankfurt and Paris, before ending up in Portugal, contemplating yet a further move, to South America, changing manner and name as the situation requires. Wherever he chooses to live, he is (unlike so many of Mann's early heroes) fully at home in the social sphere, whose customs, foibles, desires and vanities he quickly masters. Like so many other picaresque characters of European fiction, from Grimmelhausen's Simplissisimus through to Defoe's Moll Flanders and Fielding's Tom Jones, Krull lives according to the rule of self-interest and personal gain, not morality or scruple. His philosophy is summed up towards the end of the novel when, dismissing his reservations about the authenticity of the Marquis' drawing style, he concludes: 'whether this procedure was artistic or fraudulent I was not called upon to say, but I decided at once that, cheating or no, it was something I could do'.[235] Like his picaresque predecessors, Krull possesses an irrepressible faith in his ability to master circumstances, seeing the world as a challenge to be met, a problem to be solved. After the death of his father and the dissolution of the family concern, he leaves his native Rhineland and goes for the first time to Frankfurt, where he realizes that his poverty must exclude him from enjoying the many attractions of the city. His response, however, is not one of dejection, but of youthful anticipation, an eagerness which is captured in the breathless prose of the narrative: 'But his senses are lively, his mind attentive and alert; he sees, he enjoys, he assimilates; and if at first the rush of noise and faces confuses this son of a sleepy country town, bewilders him, frightens him indeed, nevertheless he possesses mother wit and strength of mind enough slowly to become master of his inner turmoil and turn it to good purpose for his education ('Bildung'), his enthusiastic researches'.[236]

Krull is a character rare in Mann's fiction: a successful blend of the introvert and the extrovert, of the intellectual and the actor, whose 'artistry' is not a symbol of an alienated consciousness (as it is in so many of Mann's earlier characters), but the expression of a highly developed confidence in his own worth

and talents. Even as a boy he is fully aware of his natural
attributes as a 'young god, slender, graceful, yet powerful in
build, with a golden skin and flawless proportions'.[237] To this
highly narcissistic self-image he adds a refinement of the senses
of sight and sound, and an 'easy courtesy and social grace' that
proves all-important in the aristocratic milieu that Krull eventually comes to inhabit. His greatest gift, however, is his
unsurpassable talent for dissimulation and impersonation. Krull
is born into a world of deception and play-acting. The family
home, a villa built around a fantasy architecture of grottoes,
distorting mirrors and fake doors is frequently the scene of
Bacchanalian orgies, of 'feasting, dancing, piano-playing, rough-
housing' enjoyed by parents and guests alike in a spirit of
hedonistic excess, overseen by the arch-sensualist and *roué*,
Krull senior. This is a world of inveterate deception: moral,
sexual and social. Even the supposedly high class 'champagne',
*Loreley, extra cuvée*, which is packed in the most extravagant way
by Krull's father, turns out to be a vinicultural impostor, an un-
palatable concoction closer to 'petroleum or fusel oil' than wine.
That the family business also turns out to be a financial fraud
seems to lie in the very nature of things.

The theatrical propensity that Krull inherits from his familial
background is further reinforced by another family member: the
artistic godfather, 'Professor' Schimmelpreester. It is Schimmelpreester who, relating the classical Greek story of Pericles and
the light-figured sculptor, Pheidias, first establishes in Krull's
mind the affinity between the artist and the criminal. It is also
Schimelpreester who first awakens Krull's enjoyment of play-
acting and masquerading. Dressed up in all sorts of costumes,
Krull begins to develop a feeling for his own protean self and an
appreciation of the magical properties of impersonation and
dissimulation: 'with the aid of costume and wig I seemed not
only able to put on whatever social rank or personal characteristics I chose, but could actually adapt myself to any given
period or century'.[238] This insight into the social profit of
disguise is further reinforced by his first visit to the real stage of
his local playhouse. Here, in this 'realm of brightness and
beauty', willed into existence by the creative imagination, Krull
learns to appreciate the complex psychology of deception. At its
centre is the actor, Müller-Rosé, who provides the focus of
adoration for an audience held in awe by the 'magic' of his

personality, as he adapts himself to the many roles he is asked to perform in a plot that is 'audacious, adventurous, and *risqué*, by turns'. Although the young Krull, glimpsing the reality back-stage, discovers that beneath this charismatic persona lies a 'repulsive little worm', his admiration for the bluff that has been sublimely achieved remains undiminished. Mann had, once before, written about the realm of the theatrical personality and its hold over the spectator, in his political allegory, *Mario and the Magician*, published in 1930. In that story, the narrator learns that passive viewing can provide no resistance to the determined and charismatic personality. Krull learns something similar from his scrutiny of the actor: that the human race is possessed of a desire to believe in fiction and that the actor and his audience are bound together in a bond of mutual dependence, an insight that will later inform Krull's own 'performances' as a confidence trickster.[239]

Krull comes to live a life governed by dissimulation and learns to play a variety of roles: the invalid (for his school teachers and family doctor), an epileptic (for the army draft board), a pimp (for the prostitute, Rozsa), a polyglot (for the Parisian hotel manager), the menial lift-boy (for the hotel's clientele), the gigolo (for the wealthy heiress) and finally, his greatest role of all, the aristocrat (for the Marquis de Venosta). In taking on these personae, Krull never loses sight of the material gains that might accrue to him through their successful execution; as the episode with Madame Houpflé's necklace indicates, he is fully aware of the importance of money in the world, and has few scruples about taking advantage of lucrative situations. And yet his confidence tricks are not simply aimed at material acquisition. In this respect he differs from his forerunners in the picaresque tradition. Krull views his life as much as a game or work of art, as a struggle for survival. Indeed, he deliberately refuses to choose those avenues of personal advancement that would offer him a high and secure standard of living precisely because they would curtail the playful nature of his existence. Thus the invitations to companionship made both by Miss Twentyman and Lord Strathbogie are politely refused in favour of a life that can be lived according to the 'free play and dreams, self-created and self-sufficient, dependent, that is, only on imagination' ('Phantasie').[240] When he finally does accept the suggestion that he exchange places with the Marquis de Venosta, so that the

latter will be free to live as he pleases with his actress consort,
Zaza, away from the scrutiny of his disapproving parents, Krull
accepts the offer because, like any actor, he welcomes the chance to
play a new role. For him, it is almost as if he is taking part in one of
those stories so dear to the childhood reader, of 'disguise and
recognition' ('Einkleidungs – und Erhöhungsgeschichten').[241]
It is a decision taken out of aesthetic rather than pragmatic
considerations.

Nowhere is this feeling for the playful quality of experience
more in evidence than in the confidence trickster's role as lover.
His physical self-mastery, beauty of form and a facility for play-
acting combine to produce a talent that assures his success in
this area. The origins of Krull's 'gifts for the pleasures of love' lie
(as with his more general propensity towards artifice and
dramatic performance) in his parents' household. It is not only
to alcoholic or culinary excesses that the Krulls give themselves
over during the course of their extended 'parties'; their 'mindless
gluttony' around the dinner table is more than matched by a
taste for sexual indulgence that evinces itself in the unusual
relationship between Frau Krull and her teenage daughter, as
well as in the more mundane activities that the pair undertake
with visiting tradesmen. In such a climate, it is hardly surprising
that the young Krull, so precocious in other respects, should seek
to add sexual conquest to his many other physical accomplish-
ments. His experiences with the house-maid Genovefa are in
keeping with the bawdy element that has adhered to the
picaresque novel from its very beginnings and Krull, as the
narrator, reproduces the adventure in the familiar rhetoric of
transport and delight common to the genre. Yet this encounter
involves, for Krull, more than just the satisfaction of curiosity
and aroused desire; far from being his first step on the road
towards being a 'lady-killer', the experience enjoyed in the arms
of Genovefa leads him into a process of speculation about the
psychology of desire and the need to retain a distance from what
he terms, in a characteristically condescending way, the 'limited
and illusionary satisfaction of appetite' ('des Verlangens').[242]

What Krull learns from his experience with Genovefa is that
sex without phantasy is an animal rather than human activity.
And this insight informs his second amorous encounter, with the
exotic 'lady of pleasure', Rozsa, during his Frankfurt period.
From the very first meeting, an element of 'pantomime' pervades

their relationship. This is highly apt, because Rozsa, the ex-circus performer, has, in her new career, come to exchange one set of 'arts' for another. On the occasions of their greatest intimacy, Rozsa, like all true artists, dispenses with explanations or justifications, engrossing herself instead in her performance. As Krull relates, 'conversations played a very minor role in our association, for Rozsa restricted herself to simple, practical directions and commands, accompanied by short, excited cries, which were survivals from her earliest youth – that is, from the circus ring'.[243]

In the 'hands' of Rozsa, 'this exacting and beloved mistress', Krull makes the transition from sex to eroticism in his amorous education. The lessons he learns in 'Rozsa's naughty school of love' stand him in good stead for his third and most important sexual conquest: that of the wealthy heiress, Madame Houpflé. This is the same Madame Houpflé who had unwittingly been the donor of the diamond necklace that had first provided Krull with the means to raise himself from his lowly position as kitchen hand and lift-boy in the Parisian hotel. The chance meeting of Krull with Madame Houpflé in the Hotel Saint James and Albany must be seen as one of those happy coincidences that frequently befalls the hero of the picaresque novel: it is fortune favouring the brave. He helps her out of the lift and is invited to her room. Unlike Rozsa, Madame Houpflé is a poetess, both by profession and inclination, with the habit of putting 'everything into words'. What she achieves through her poetic discourse is the transformation of sexual seduction into an erotic theatrical performance. Roles become reversed: Krull is no longer the cocky lift-boy, but the 'suave god, Hermes', at once thief, master and lover, while she, the original wealthy benefactress, becomes slave, whore and, finally, willing victim of crime, as Krull, adding material gain to sensual gratification, makes off into the night with her valuables. Their amorous encounter involves, in fact, an excess of play-acting; the confidence man is, for once, out-trumped in role playing and forced to dissimulate more than he wishes. In this seduction, it is difficult to tell who is the victim and who the victimizer: the deceiver and deceived have become willing partners in an act of mutual deception.

Krull seeks from such experiences, however, more than mere material gain. For what really motivates Mann's hero is not advancement for its own sake, but as the means of obtaining

what, even at an early stage in his life, he calls 'the joy of life', a
feeling for the fullness of the world's offerings, a 'precious and
painful feeling, compounded of envy, yearning, hope, and love,
that the sight of beauty and light-hearted perfection kindles in
the souls of men'.[244] Krull's play-acting and will to dissimulation is not simply the tool of a careerist; it is also the product of a
highly refined aesthetic sensibility. This sensibility is evident in
his response to his very first misdemeanour: the theft from the
local delicatessen. In spite of the undeniable culpability of the
act, this is an incident which is, in itself, banal, a case of minor
pilfering. What raises it from the realm of petty criminality is the
sheer delight and intensity of emotion that the sight of the edible
cornucopia produces in the juvenile offender: 'It was indeed
either a fairy-tale or a dream! Everyday laws and prosaic
regulations were all suspended. One might give free rein to one's
desires and let imagination roam in blissful unrestraint. So great
was the joy of beholding this bountiful spot completely at my
disposal that I felt my legs begin to jerk and twitch. It took great
self-control not to burst into a cry of joy at so much newness and
freedom'.[245]

Krull must be seen, then, as something more than merely a
modern version of the classic picaresque hero. He is a character
who brings such an intensity and refinement of feeling to his
enjoyment of the world that the latter becomes, like the moment
in the delicatessen, transformed into an aesthetic object. Krull
elevates confidence trickery to an art form and, in doing so,
transcends the base criminality that adheres to that fraudulent
activity. As such, he is like the many other 'artistic' figures who
appear throughout the novel: his godfather Schimmelpreester,
the actor Müller-Rosé and even the circus star, Andromache.
Watching the daredevil flights of this nimble trapeze artist, who
employs only the most basic of props, Krull is led to speculate on
how the gifted individual is able to dispense with the gross
animal heritage of nature: 'it is between animal and angel, so I
reflected, that man takes his stand. His place is closer to the
animals, that we must admit. But she, my adored one, though all
body, was a chaster body, untainted by humanity, and stood
much closer to the angels'.[246]

Krull's celebration of the achievements of Andromache echoes
the sentiments of one of Mann's greatest intellectual mentors:
Friedrich Nietzsche. The influence of that great German philo-

sopher had been evident in much of Mann's early fiction, from *Buddenbrooks* through to *Death in Venice*, appearing wherever the themes of decadence, knowledge and self formation had been addressed. The influence of Nietzsche appears again in *Krull*, but, characteristically, in a lighter and less metaphysical form, as an exponent of physical harmony and grace. Indeed, the very concept of the Superman (Übermensch), which Nietzsche first projected in his spiritual allegory, *Thus spake Zarathustra* (1885), to define those rare individuals who can find the source of truth and morality within themselves, parallels Mann's own estimation of Krull and other 'such exquisite and well formed people [who] sense in themselves a kind of apotheosis of the body'.[247]

Krull's emphasis upon the body and the senses has, indeed, a higher purpose. When, later in the novel, he asks of the attractive and precociously cynical Zouzou, Professor Kuckuck's daughter, 'What would become of life and what would become of joy – without which there can be no life – if appearance and the surface world of the senses no longer counted for anything?'[248] he is not only clarifying the creed by which he has lived throughout his short life, he is also giving expression to an underlying philosophical theme in the novel. The fullest elaboration of this theme is, significantly, given to Professor Kuckuck (who becomes Krull's final mentor). Kuckuck's research into Paleo-Zoology has led him to speculate upon the transitory nature of existence and man's place within this scheme of things. Kuckuck is not a nihilist, but (along with Nietzsche) he realizes that human life may have no other purpose than the assertion and perfection of itself. He adds: 'There was no question [. . .] that Life on earth was not only an ephemeral episode, but *Being in itself was also* – an interlude between Nothingness and Nothingness'.[249] In spite of the abstruse nature of Kuckuck's speculations, they are in keeping with an essential tenet of Krull's own more practical philosophy of life: there is no other purpose to creation than the perfection of self.

Krull views his many performances as just so many opportunities for self-expression: they are part of an elaborate 'game', which is pursued purely for the sheer delights of incognito that it offers. The success of this game, however, is only made possible because society is dominated by the same aesthetics of play and play-acting which reign within the world of the theatre. This is,

certainly, not a new insight and when Krull reflects on how easy
an 'interchangeability' of master and servant would be were he
and the Marquis de Venosta to exchange garments he is doing little
more than giving expression to the age old adage that 'clothes
maketh the man'.[250] After all, Krull has been such a success in
his many 'performances' precisely because he *looks* the part.

On other occasions, however, this insight into the fictional
component of social behaviour is extended to the realm of
personality itself, to allow a much more sophisticated analysis of
the relationship between play-acting and individual identity to
emerge. It is here that Mann's novel comes closest to other
works of the modernist period, such as Gide's *The Counterfeiters*
(1926), and even to the more recent post-modernist fiction of
Italo Calvino, Vladimir Nabokov and Jorge Luis Borges, writers
who explored 'the problematical relationship of the [. . .] hero to
the systems in which he finds himself and the fictions which
surround him'.[251] As in the work of these writers, *The Confessions of Felix Krull* explores the notion that personality is a
fiction, something artificially constructed. When Krull, for example, finally agrees to take on the job of impersonating the
Marquis de Venosta, he does so not purely on account of the
material gains that will accrue from impersonating so dis-
tinguished a person, but for the pleasure of renewing the source
of his individual self: 'it was the change and renewal of my worn-
out self, the fact that I had been able to put off the old Adam and
slip on a new, that gave me such a sense of fulfilment and
happiness'.[252] It is not simply that Krull has the facility to put
on a mask to dissimulate the real self beneath; this real self is
itself a fiction, an entity whose production and maintenance
requires a perpetual exertion of the will. When, coming towards
the end of his period as a hotel servant, and already wealthy
enough to pass himself off as an aristocrat, he asks himself which
role is a masquerade and which a reality, he concludes that both
were simply performances and that 'behind the two appearances, the real I ('das ich-selber-Sein') could not be identified
because it actually did not exist'.[253]

There is one final area in which this highly modern notion of
the primacy of fiction is evident: in Krull's narrative itself.
Because of the personal and intimate nature of the experiences
with which it dealt, the picaresque novel had conventionally
been related in the first-person, and often in the form of a

memoir. Such a mode of narration was intended to support the impression that the text was a direct account of the experiences rendered. Mann retains this narrative convention but undermines its pretence to authenticity by showing that Krull's narrative also partakes of that quality of playful dissimulation that is a feature of his dubious activities. Krull not only puts the most positive gloss upon his many misdemeanours, representing the consequence of lies, deceits and thefts as the fruits of an artistic nature. The reader's confidence in the much vaunted truthfulness of Krull's narrative is playfully undermined from beginning to end by the admission of inconsistencies and contradictions: the initial contention that his memoirs are supposedly not written for publication is, he later admits, blatantly false; an early dismissal of the laws of art is later contradicted by his commitment to the 'conventions of writing'; and, finally, his very account of his own story is vitiated by being filtered through a memory which is (as he admits) 'faded' and unreliable.[254]

It is, above all, Krull's often voiced mistrust of language that proves the final obstacle to the reader's reliance on him as a narrator. For, in spite of his own eloquence and indisputable way with words, Krull regards language as a 'cool, prosaic device, that first begetter of tame, mediocre morality, so essentially alien to the hot, inarticulate realm of nature'.[255] The true realm of self-expression is that of the body, a province where Krull, confidence trickster and actor on the social stage, excels. 'Speech is the foe of mystery' and it is mystery which is appreciated by the romantic Krull above all else, not only because, like the garment loosely hung on Rozsa or Madame Houpflé, it bestows an erotic dimension on desire, but also, because it labels and categorizes, and, hence, removes the aura surrounding his many 'creative' deeds, naming them for what they are: acts of a determined con-man. For that reason, the reader learns only as much about Krull, his motivation, goals and values, as that chameleon rogue wishes to reveal. In the final analysis, the process of narration produced in the novel can itself be seen as an elaborate act of deception played, this time, upon the final and most unsuspecting victim of Krull's confidence trickery: the reader.

At one crucial point in his story, Krull, faced with the possibility of destitution after the death of his father and the dissolution of the family firm, is offered the chance of becoming a hotel waiter in Paris. The prospect of escaping from his 'cramped and odious native place' ('gehäßigte Enge der Heimat') into the 'great world' beyond fills Krull with 'ecstasy', as he anticipates liberation and the vital expansiveness that will indeed come to characterize his wayward but sunny life.[256] It is this same openness to experience which finds expression in Mann's final novel, and which makes it such a remarkable achievement. In *The Confessions of Felix Krull*, the grim legacy of German Romanticism, its introspection, mysticism and a sympathy with death, has been finally overcome. Krull's self-command and superior understanding lead him not into irony (and that distance from the world suffered by so many of Mann's earlier heroes), but to sociability and a happy integration. *Felix Krull* is one of the few of Mann's novels not to end in death, but in the social and bodily fulfilment of its hero, as Krull finds himself welcomed into Professor Kuckuck's family and into the arms of the professor's wife. Like that other great modernist novel, James Joyce's *Ulysses*, Mann's novel also ends on a note of orgiastic pleasure which is a metaphor for the hero's embracing of life. His advances to the daughter, Zouzou, spurned, Krull finds himself quite suddenly together with the mother whose passion is beyond containment, and whose consummation brings together the central motifs of the novel: the unity of sexuality and play: ' "Holé! Heho! Ahé!" she exclaimed in majestic jubilation. A whirlwind of primordial forces seized and bore me into the realm of ecstasy. And high and stormy, under ardent caresses, stormier than at the Iberian game of blood, I saw the surging of that queenly bosom'.[257]

# 10

# Conclusion: Thomas Mann: A Modern Novelist?

In this study of the fiction of Thomas Mann, I have attempted to introduce the reader to the major works of that author and have concentrated largely upon the texts themselves, discussing the fiction of other novelists only where necessary. In a series devoted to the modern novel, it would, however, not be out of place, in the way of conclusion, to consider Mann in the context of other great novelists of the modernist period, such as Joyce, Proust or Kafka, and to ask the obvious question: how *modern* was his writing when compared to their fiction?

When Mann started writing in the last decade of the nineteenth century, European literature was on the point of breaking with the traditions of the great Realist novel and embracing the more experimental aesthetics of Modernism. The novels of, in particular, Joyce, Proust and Kafka opened up in their different ways radically new perspectives on the art of novel writing. Mann was certainly aware of the work of these writers, but it is difficult to talk of direct influence. In spite of his extended use of the stream of consciousness technique in one of the chapters of *Lotte in Weimar*, Mann did not read the fiction of Joyce until late in his career, and even then it was not in the original English. The same is true of his knowledge of Proust. There is little indication that Mann had read Proust before 1935, and it is certain that he had not read Proust by 1924, the year in which he published *The Magic Mountain*, a novel which also explores the varieties of ways in which time can be appropriated by individual consciousness.[258] Mann was certainly more familiar with the great names of German Modernism, such as Rilke, Kafka, Musil and Hesse (with whom he developed a long friendship), but his comments upon their work are often politely appreciative rather than enthusiastic. Mann devoted his greatest literary-critical energies to writing about the great names of nineteenth rather than twentieth-century literature: Storm, Stifter and, above all, Fontane.[259] Mann inherited from such writers a familiarity with the conventions of nineteenth-century Realism, which included psychological and 'rounded' characterization, the ability to develop a linear and consequential plot, and a narrative point of view capable of registering the detail and variety of the external world. The benefits of this heritage became immediately evident in Mann's first novel, *Buddenbrooks* (1901), whose epic combination of the individual and the social stands in favourable comparison with any of the great Realist novels of the nineteenth century.

From the German Romantics, however, Mann got something equally valuable: an awareness of the symbolic nature of the physical world (evident in his widespread use of the device of the *leit-motif*), and a sensitivity for the mystical and transcendent aspects of experience (particularly as they manifest themselves through the medium of music). Romanticism, both as a loosely knit series of philosophical ideas and as a literary form, pervades Mann's work. It is evident, for example, in *The Magic Mountain* (1924), a novel that is set in a magical realm where the laws governing time and space seem suspended. The sense of time-lessness which reigns in the sanatorium owes more to the Romantic world of the Venusberg or to the eternal present evoked in the poetic fiction of Novalis' *Heinrich von Ofterdingen* (1802) than it does to modern notions about the relativity of experience. Likewise in *Death in Venice*, the spectral figures who act as premonitions of Aschenbach's decline and eventual death occupy a strange literary no-man's-land; they are not realistic characters, and yet they are certainly much more than figments of his imagination. They are, in fact, the descendants of characters who appear in Romantic *Märchen*, such as Ludwig Tieck's 'Der blonde Eckbert' (1797) and 'Der Runenberg' (1804), modern-day *Doppelgänger*, who embody certain fateful aspects of the hero's personality.

Finally, both traditions, the Realist and the Romantic, come together in that genre of the novel that Mann favoured above all others: the *Bildungs* or *Künstlerroman* (the novel of formation or artistic development). Mann himself viewed *The Magic Moun-*

tain as a parody of the *Bildungsroman*, but the focus of that genre upon personal experience and the intellectual growth of the individual is evident in novels as different as *Doctor Faustus* (1947) and *The Confessions of Felix Krull* (1955). Both chart a conflict between individual and society, and speculate on the ways that this conflict can be resolved (negatively, in the case of the former novel, and positively, in the case of the latter).

In the light of these powerful nineteenth-century influences, the question still remains: what is distinctively *modern* about Mann's fiction? The question can only be partially answered by looking at the style of his novels. Compared to other modern writers such as Joyce or Kafka, Mann's work can seem stylistically conservative. With his convoluted sentence structures and often erudite vocabulary, his linguistic register is an elevated one, and clearly presupposes an educated readership capable of appreciating the many cultural and philosophical allusions that abound in novels such as *The Magic Mountain* and *Doctor Faustus*. It is a style that lends support to Mann's self-image as a 'man of letters', and many of his younger and more radical contemporaries, such as the Marxist playwright, Bertolt Brecht, regarded such a self-image as indicative of Mann's essential conservatism, even in those periods in which Mann consciously espoused a social democratic political line. Mann, however, could be stylistically inventive, and many critics have pointed to the 'musical' structure of his fiction, its use of formal repetition (most evident in the *leit-motif* device) and its employment of the montage technique (which allows diverse and often non-literary materials to be incorporated into the narrative) as evidence of a desire to revise the conventions of the nineteenth-century novel.

Mann's greatest contribution to the modern novel lies, however, in the fact that he explored a number of themes that stand at the centre of the intellectual self-understanding of our age: the relationship between knowledge and morality; the perpetual threat of the irrational, and the difficulty in resisting its appeal, particularly in its aesthetic and political manifestations; the amorphous nature of sexuality; and the fluid nature of the self and personal identity. It is Mann's preoccupation with these themes throughout a period of more than half a century of writing that gives a sense of continuity to his corpus. Above all, Mann's work is pervaded by a sense of crisis, which is typical of much of the modern literature of our period. In Mann's case, it arose from a feeling that the values and traditions of the class to which he belonged (the educated bourgeoisie or *Bildungsbürgertum*) was proving unable to deal with the moral, social and political problems posed by the new age of mass society. That sense of crisis is particularly evident in *Mario and the Magician* (1930), where the narrator (who is very much an embodiment of *Bildungsbürgertum*) ends up merely as a passive observer of fascist charisma, forced to find a purely vicarious consolation in its bloody termination by the young worker, Mario.

The narrator of the story is, in fact, both a representative of the *Bürgertum* and an alter ego of Mann and, as such, points to one of the greatest strengths and one of the most modern components of Mann's writing: his ability to disperse himself across a number of identities in his fiction, speaking through personae who often voice quite opposing views on the world. His novels are often the site of a philosophical struggle or dialectic: between Naphta and Settembrini in *The Magic Mountain*, between Joseph and his brothers in Mann's Biblical story and even between Thomas and Christian Buddenbrook in *Buddenbrooks*. Mann's widespread use of irony in these novels makes it futile for the reader to look for a clear resolution to these intellectual confrontations. Mann does not allow us to come down entirely on the side of one character rather than an other, because knowledge is not for Mann (or for his mentor, Nietzsche) an absolute state but a process that is of value because it is open-ended. In the final analysis, it is precisely this unresolved nature of Mann's fiction, the fact that it posits a world that is perpetually open, both for the characters and, in the process of interpretation, for the reader, that makes Thomas Mann one of the quintessential novelists of the modern period.

# Notes

1. Thomas Mann, *A Sketch of My Life*, translated from the German by H. T. Lowe-Porter (New York, 1970), p. 74.
2. See Hans Bürgin and Hans-Otto Mayer, *Thomas Mann: A Chronicle of his Life* (Alabama, 1969), p. 1.
3. *A Sketch of My Life*, op. cit., pp. 3–4.
4. Quoted from Hans Bürgin and Hans-Otto Mayer, op. cit., p. 20.
5. Ibid, pp. 18–19.
6. See, for example, his diary entry for 30 March 1919, in Thomas Mann, *Diaries for 1918–1939*, translated from the German by Richard and Clara Winston, selection and foreword by Hermann Kesten (New York, 1982), p. 42. What Mann termed his 'sexual inversion' seems to have reached a critical point in 1920, as is shown by an entry for 14 July. See ibid, p. 101.
7. See *The Letters of Thomas Mann*, selected and translated by Richard and Clara Winston (Harmondsworth, 1975), p. 69.
8. The history of this tense relationship between the two brothers at this time has been well charted by Marcel Reich-Ranicki in his *The King and his Rival* (Bonn, 1985).
9. See Thomas Mann, *Reflections of a Nonpolitical Man*, translated, and with an introduction by Walter D. Morris (New York, 1983), p. 2. The original German edition was first published in 1918.
10. Mann's refutation of these accusations was published in a short article in *Die Literarische Welt*, 4 (24 February 1928), p. 1.
11. See Thomas Mann, 'Mario and the Magician', in *Mario and the Magician and other Stories* (Penguin edition, Harmondsworth, 1975), p. 150. For the German source, see Thomas Mann, 'Mario und der Zauberer', in *Die Erzählungen, 2 Bände* (Fischer Bücherei, Frankfurt am Main, 1967), Vol. 2, pp. 535–536.
12. *The Letters of Thomas Mann*, op. cit., pp. 167–168 (p. 168).
13. See his diary entry for 3 September 1933 in Thomas Mann, *Diaries for 1918–1939*, op. cit., p. 168.
14. See his diary entry for 31 December 1933, ibid, pp. 186–187 (p. 186).
15. See his letter of 7 June 1954 to daughter Erika in *The Letters of Thomas Mann*, op cit., pp. 464–467 (p. 465).
16. Mann entered into a lively debate with a number of such 'inner emigrants' to justify his position. The documentation has been collected

by J. F. G. Grosser in his *Die große Kontroverse* (Hamburg, 1963).

17. This was the assessment of *Time* magazine. See Klaus Schröter (ed.), *Thomas Mann im Urteil seiner Zeit: Dokumente, 1891–1955* (Hamburg, 1969), pp. 445–447 (p. 447).

18. See Hans Erich Nossack, 'Inbegriff der Unehrlichkeit and Feigheit', in Marcel Reich-Ranicki (ed.), *Was halten Sie von Thomas Mann?: Achtzehn Autoren antworten* (Frankfurt am Main, 1986), pp. 67–68 (p. 67). (My translation).

19. See Thomas Mann, *Reflections of a Nonpolitical Man*, translated, and with an introduction, by Walter D. Morris (New York, 1983), pp. 98. The original German edition was first published in 1918.

20. Ibid, p. 98.

21. Thus Ernest K. Bramsted, *Aristocracy and the Middle-Classes in Germany: Social Types in German Literature, 1830–1900* (Chicago, 1964), p. 201.

22. Thomas Mann, *Buddenbrooks: The Decline of a Family* (Penguin edition, Harmondsworth, 1957), p. 44. For the German source, see Thomas Mann, *Buddenbrooks: Verfall einer Familie* (Fischer Taschenbuch, Frankfurt am Main, 1960), p. 39. Subsequent references are to both editions.

23. See the entry on 'Biedermeier' in Henry and Mary Garland (eds.), *The Oxford Companion to German Literature* (Oxford, 1976), pp. 81–82.

24. *Buddenbrooks*, op. cit., p. 88; (p. 78).

25. Ibid, p. 83; (p. 73).

26. Ibid, p. 404; (pp. 355–356).

27. Ibid, p. 48; (p. 43).

28. Ibid, p. 135; (p. 120).

29. Ibid, p. 160; (p. 142).

30. Ibid, p. 88; (p. 78).

31. Ibid, p. 207; (p. 184).

32. Ibid, p. 353; (p. 310).

33. Ibid, p. 353; (p. 310).

34. Ibid, p. 13; (p. 13).

35. Ibid, p. 521; (p. 460).

36. Ibid, p. 15; (p. 14).

37. Ibid, p. 474; (p. 419).

38. Ibid, pp. 506–507; (pp. 447–448).

39. See, for example, pp. 543 and 574; (pp. 478 and 506).

40. Ibid, p. 580; (p. 511).

41. Ibid, p. 364; (pp. 319–320).

42. Ernst Haeckel is quoted by Alfred Kelly, *The Descent of Darwin: The Popularization of Darwinism in Germany, 1860–1914* (Chapel Hill, 1981), p. 22.

43. See Thomas Mann, *Reflections of a Nonpolitical Man*, translated, and with an introduction, by Walter D. Morris (New York, 1983), p. 12. (I have preferred my translation here.)

44. *Reflections of a Nonpolitical Man*, op. cit., p. 49.

45. *Buddenbrooks*, op. cit., pp. 580–583; (pp. 511–514).

46. Ibid, p. 22; (p. 20).

47. Ibid, p. 375; (p. 329).

48. Ibid, p. 9; (p. 9).

49. Ibid, p. 487; (p. 431).
50. Ibid, p. 558; (p. 492). See also Friedrich Nietzsche, *Twilight of the Idols* (Penguin edition, 1972), p. 60.
51. See Thomas Mann, *Reflections of a Nonpolitical Man*, translated, and with an introduction, by Walter D. Morris (New York, 1983), p. 67. The original German edition was first published in 1918.
52. See Thomas Mann, *Little Herr Friedemann and Other Stories* (Penguin edition, Harmondsworth, 1972), p. 30. For the German source, see Thomas Mann, *Die Erzählungen, 2 Bände* (Fischer Bücherei, Frankfurt am Main, 1967), Vol. 1, p. 73. Subsequent references are to both editions.
53. Ibid, p. 35; (p. 78).
54. Ibid, p. 16; (p. 60).
55. Ibid, p. 98; (p. 146).
56. Ibid, p. 60; (p. 103).
57. Ibid, p. 59; (p. 103).
58. Ibid, p. 129; (p. 262).
59. Ibid, p. 143; (p. 275).
60. Ibid, p. 149; (p. 280).
61. Ibid, p. 150; (p. 281).
62. Ibid, p. 156; (p. 287).
63. See Thomas Mann, 'Tristan' in *Death in Venice, Tristan and Tonio Kröger*, (Penguin edition, Harmondsworth, 1955), p. 113. For the German source, see Thomas Mann, *Die Erzählungen, 2 Bände* (Fischer Bücherei, Frankfurt am Main, 1967), Vol. 1, p. 186. Subsequent references are to both editions.
64. Ibid, p. 121; (p. 192).
65. Ibid, p. 128; (p. 198).
66. Thomas Mann, *Little Herr Friedemann and Other Stories* (Penguin edition, Harmondsworth, 1972), p. 103. For the German source, see Thomas Mann, *Die Erzählungen, 2 Bände* (Fischer Bücherei, Frankfurt am Main, 1967), Vol. 1, p. 201.
67. See Thomas Mann, 'Tonio Kröger' in *Death in Venice, Tristan and Tonio Kröger*, (Penguin edition, Harmondsworth, 1955), p. 147. For the German source, see Thomas Mann, *Die Erzählungen, 2 Bände* (Fischer Bücherei, Frankfurt am Main, 1967), Vol. 1, p. 219. Subsequent references are to both editions.
68. Ibid, p. 148; (p. 220).
69. Ibid, pp. 153–154; (p. 225).
70. Ibid, p. 161; (p. 231).
71. Ibid, p. 171; (p. 239).
72. Ibid, p. 187; (p. 253).
73. Ibid, pp. 190–191; (p. 255).
74. See *The Letters of Thomas Mann*, selected and translated by Richard and Clara Winston (Harmondsworth, 1975), p. 46.
75. See, for example, Richard Schaukal, 'Thomas Mann: Ein liter-psychologisches Porträt', first published in 1903 and reprinted in Klaus Schröter (ed.), *Thomas Mann im Urteil seiner Zeit: Dokumente, 1891–1955* (Hamburg, 1969), pp. 27–28.
76. See *The Letters of Thomas Mann*, op. cit., p. 112.

77. Thomas Mann, 'Death in Venice' in *Death in Venice, Tristan and Tonio Kröger*, (Penguin edition, Harmondsworth, 1955), p. 19. For the German source, see Thomas Mann, *Die Erzählungen, 2 Bände* (Fischer Bücherei, Frankfurt am Main, 1967), Vol. 1, p. 347. Subsequent references are to both editions.

78. Ibid, p. 12; (p. 342).

79. Ibid, p. 17; (p. 346).

80. See Thomas Mann, *Buddenbrooks: The Decline of a Family* (Penguin edition, Harmondsworth, 1957), p. 558. For the German source, see *Buddenbrooks: Verfall einer Familie* (Fischer Taschenbuch, Frankfurt am Main, 1960), p. 492.

81. *Death in Venice*, p. 18; (p. 347).

82. *Letters*, op. cit., p. 48.

83. *Death in Venice*, p. 16; (p. 345).

84. See Friedrich Nietzsche, *The Birth of Tragedy*, translated by Francis Golffing (New York, 1956), p. 19.

85. *Death in Venice*, p. 43; (p. 367).

86. Ibid, p. 9; (p. 340).

87. This is how Mann interpreted Aschenbach's feelings in the essay 'On Myself', first published in 1940 and republished in *Dichter über ihre Dichtungen*, Volume VI/1, *Thomas Mann, Part I: 1889–1917*, edited by Hans Wysling, with Marianne Fischer (Passau, 1975), pp. 438–442 (p. 439).

88. *Death in Venice*, p. 910; and p. 340.

89. Ibid, p. 27; (p. 354).

90. See Thomas Mann, 'Tonio Kröger' in *Death in Venice, Tristan and Tonio Kröger*, (Penguin edition, Harmondsworth, 1955), p. 183. For the German source, see Thomas Mann, *Die Erzählungen, 2 Bände* (Fischer Bücherei, Frankfurt am Main, 1967), Vol. 1, p. 249.

91. See Thomas Mann, *Reflections of a Nonpolitical Man*, translated, and with an introduction, by Walter D. Morris (New York, 1983), pp. 422–423.

92. *Death in Venice*, p. 54; (p. 376).

93. Ibid, p. 33; (p. 359).

94. Ibid, p. 61; (p. 381).

95. Ibid, p. 54; (p. 376).

96. Ibid, p. 67; (p. 386).

97. Ibid, p. 74; (p. 393).

98. Ibid, p. 76; (p. 394).

99. See Thomas Mann, *Reflections of a Nonpolitical Man*, translated, and with an introduction, by Walter D. Morris (New York, 1983), p. 153. The original German edition was first published in 1918.

100. *Death in Venice*, p. 7; (p. 338).

101. See Mann's 'Tischrede bei der Feier der fünfzigsten Geburtstags', given in 1925 and republished in *Dichter über ihre Dichtungen*, Volume VI/1, *Thomas Mann, Part I: 1889–1917*, edited by Hans Wysling, with Marianne Fischer (Passau, 1975), p. 500. (My translation).

102. See Mann's letter to Paul Amann in August 1915. Reprinted in Wysling ibid., pp. 455–456 (p. 455). (My translation).

103. Thomas Mann, *The Magic Mountain* Penguin edition, Harmondsworth,

1960), p. 27. For the German source, see Thomas Mann, *Der Zauberberg*, (Fischer Taschenbuch, Frankfurt am Main, 1967), p. 31. Subsequent references are to both editions.

104. Ibid, p. 183; (p. 195).
105. Ibid, p. 10; (p. 15).
106. Ibid, p. 81; (p. 87).
107. Ibid, pp. 120–121; (pp. 127–128).
108. Ibid, p. 342; (pp. 361–362).
109. Ibid, p. 81; (p. 87).
110. Ibid, p. 103; (p. 109).
111. Ibid, p. 97; (p. 103).
112. See 'zur Begrüßung Gerhart Hauptmanns in München', first published in 1926 and republished in Wysling, op. cit., pp. 521–522 (p. 522). (My translation).
113. Quoted from Martin Swales, *The German Bildungsroman from Wieland to Hesse* (Princeton, 1978), p. 3.
114. Ibid, p. 654; (p. 692).
115. Ibid, p. 57; (p. 62).
116. Ibid, p. 461; (p. 485).
117. Ibid, p. 477; (p. 502).
118. Ibid, p. 479; (p. 504).
119. Ibid, p. 485; (p. 511).
120. Ibid, p. 492; (p. 519).
121. Ibid, pp. 496–497; (p. 523). The italics are Mann's.
122. Ibid, p. 583; (pp. 616–617).
123. Ibid, p. 603; (p. 637).
124. Ibid, p. 646; (p. 684).
125. Ibid, p. 652; (p. 690).
126. From *The Letters of Thomas Mann*, selected and translated by Richard and Clara Winston (Harmondsworth, 1975), pp. 136–137 (p. 137).
127. *The Magic Mountain*, p. 716; (p. 757).
128. Ibid, p. 716: (and p. 757).
129. See 'Thomas Mann in einem Gespräch mit Bernard Guillemin', first published in 1925 and republished in *Dichter über ihre Dichtungen*, Volume VI/1, *Thomas Mann, Part I: 1889–1917*, edited by Hans Wysling, with Marianne Fischer (Passau, 1975), pp. 506–511 (p. 507). (My translation).
130. See Thomas Mann, *The Magic Mountain*, (Penguin edition, Harmondsworth, 1960), pp. 496–497. For the German source, see Thomas Mann, *Der Zauberberg*, (Fischer Taschenbuch, Frankfurt am Main, 1967), p. 513.
131. These are the sentiments expressed in Mann's diary entry for 9 June 1919, in Thomas Mann, *Diaries for 1918–1939*, translated from the German by Richard and Clara Winston, selection and foreword by Hermann Kesten (New York, 1982), pp. 58–59 (p. 59).
132. See 'Von deutscher Republik', reprinted in *Essays*, vol. 2, *Politische Reden und Schriften*, ausgewählt, eingeleitet und erläutert von Hermann Kurzke (Frankfurt am Main, 1977), pp. 59–93 (p. 93.). My translation.
133. See 'Deutsche Ansprache: Ein Appell an die Vernunft, in *Essays*, vol. 2, *Politische Reden und Schriften*, pp. 109–125 (p. 116). My translation.

134. Ibid, p. 124.
135. Thomas Mann, 'Mario and the Magician', in *Mario and the Magician and other Stories* (Penguin edition, Harmondsworth, 1975), p. 120. For the German source, see Thomas Mann, 'Mario und der Zauberer: Ein tragisches Reiseerlebnis', in *Die Erzählungen, 2 Bände* (Fischer Bücherei, Frankfurt am Main, 1967), Vol. 2, p. 508. Subsequent references are to both editions.
136. Ibid, p. 122; (p. 510).
137. Ibid, p. 143; (p. 529).
138. Ibid, p. 133; (p. 520).
139. Ibid, p. 129; (p. 165).
140. Ibid, p. 141; (p. 527).
141. Ibid, p. 140; (p. 526).
142. Ibid, p. 133; (p. 520).
143. Ibid, p. 145; (p. 531).
144. See 'Deutsche Ansprache: Ein Appell an die Vernunft', op. cit., p. 120.
145. 'Mario and the Magician', p. 124; (p. 512).
146. Ibid, p. 150; (pp. 535–536).
147. Ibid, p. 149; (p. 534).
148. Ibid, p. 152; (p. 537).
149. See Hermann Rauschning, *The Revolution of Nihilism* (New York, 1939).
150. See his diary entry for 5 August 1934 in Thomas Mann, *Diaries for 1918–1939*, translated from the German by Richard and Clara Winston, selection and foreword by Hermann Kesten (New York, 1982), pp. 221–223 (p. 222).
151. From *The Letters of Thomas Mann*, selected and translated by Richard and Clara Winston (Harmondsworth, 1975), pp. 195–196 (p. 196). The emphasis is Mann's.
152. See Mann's letter of 1926 to Ernst Bertram in *The Letters of Thomas Mann*, op. cit., pp. 141–142 (p. 141).
153. Thomas Mann, *Joseph and his Brothers* (Penguin edition, Harmondsworth, 1978), p. 33. For the German source, see *Joseph and seine Brüder*, 3 vols (Fischer Taschenbuch Verlag, Frankfurt am Main, 1971), vol. I, p. 39. As in the Penguin edition, the pagination runs serially throughout the three volumes. Subsequent references are to both editions.
154. Ibid, p. 24; (p. 28).
155. Ibid, p. 122; (p. 139).
156. Ibid, p. 719; (p. 809).
157. Ibid, p. 389; (p. 435).
158. Ibid, p. 37; (p. 44).
159. Ibid, p. 75; (p. 87).
160. Ibid, p. 324; (p. 362).
161. Ibid, p. 389; (p. 435).
162. Ibid, p. 416; (p. 465).
163. Ibid, p. 545; (p. 608).
164. Ibid, p. 902; (p. 1021).
165. Ibid, p. 615; (p. 689).
166. Ibid, p. 817; (p. 925).
167. Ibid, p. 853; (p. 966).

168. Ibid, p. 976; (p. 1105).
169. Ibid, p. 1139; (p. 1287).
170. Ibid, p. 937; (p. 1062).
171. Ibid, p. 551; (p. 614).
172. Ibid, p. 879; (p. 997).
173. Ibid, p. 926; (p. 1049).
174. Ibid, p. 1139; (p. 1287).
175. Ibid, p. 719; (p. 810).
176. Ibid, p. 545; (p. 607). For an account of Mann's experiences in exile, see pp. 13–14 above.
177. Ibid, p. 449; (p. 499).
178. Ibid, p. 32; (pp. 37–38).
179. Ibid, p. 121; (p. 138).
180. Ibid, p. 1172; (p. 1324).
181. Ibid, p. 979; (p. 1108).
182. Ibid, p. 461; (p. 512).
183. Quoted from Hans Bürgin and Hans-Otto Mayer, *Thomas Mann: A Chronicle of his Life* (Alabama, 1969), p. 188.
184. Thomas Mann, *Lotte in Weimar* (Penguin edition, Harmondsworth, 1968), p. 245. For the German source, see Thomas Mann, *Lotte in Weimar* (Fischer Taschenbuch, Frankfurt am Main, 1959), p. 220. Subsequent references are to both editions.
185. Ibid., p. 250; (p. 225). See also Mann's diary entry for 14 October 1933 (where he expresses similar sentiments about Germany and the Nazis) in Thomas Mann, *Diaries for 1918–1939*, translated from the German by Richard and Clara Winston, selection and foreword by Hermann Kesten (New York, 1982), p. 176.
186. See 'Deutschland und die Deutschen', reprinted in *Essays*, vol. 2, *Politische Reden und Schriften*, ausgewählt, eingeleitet und erläutert von Hermann Kurzke (Frankfurt am Main, 1977), pp. 281–298 (p. 282). My translation.
187. Ibid, p. 285.
188. Ibid, pp. 285–286. Mann had analysed the morally ambiguous nature of the German tradition in music within the context of a lengthy essay on Wagner, published in the fateful year of 1933. See *Pro and Contra Wagner* (Penguin edition, 1977).
189. Thomas Mann, *Doctor Faustus: The Life of the German Composer Adrian Leverkühn as told by a Friend* (Penguin edition, Harmondsworth, 1968), p. 18. For the German source, see Thomas Mann, *Doktor Faustus: Das Leben des deutschen Tonsetzers Adrian Leverkühn erzählt von einem Freund* (Fischer Taschenbuch, Frankfurt am Main, 1971), p. 17. Subsequent references are to both editions.
190. Ibid, p. 21; (p. 20).
191. Ibid, p. 40; (p. 40).
192. Ibid, p. 55; (p. 56).
193. Ibid, p. 69; (p. 71).
194. Ibid, p. 132; (p. 135).
195. Ibid, p. 148; (p. 152).
196. Ibid, p. 151; (p. 154).

197. Ibid, p. 186; (p. 192).
198. Ibid, p. 211; (p. 218).
199. See Goethe, *Faust, Part One*, translated by Philip Wayne (Penguin edition, Harmondsworth, 1949), p. 75; and for the German source, *Goethes Faust*, kommentiert von Erich Trunz (Hamburg, 1966), p. 47.
200. *Doctor Faustus*, p. 236; (p. 244).
201. Ibid, p. 266; (p. 276).
202. Ibid, p. 351; (p. 365).
203. Ibid, p. 354; (p. 368).
204. Ibid, pp. 132–133; (p. 136).
205. Thomas Mann, *The Genesis of a Novel* (New York, 1961), p. 34.
206. *Doctor Faustus*, p. 291; (p. 302).
207. Ibid, p. 296; (p. 307).
208. Ibid, p. 319; (p. 331).
209. Ibid, p. 432; (p. 449).
210. The political philosophy of the Conservative Revolution is outlined in Jeffrey Herf, *Reactionary Modernism: Technology, Culture, and Politics in Weimar and the Third Reich* (Cambridge, 1984), pp. 18–48.
211. Ibid, p. 98; (p. 100).
212. Ibid, p. 122; (p. 125).
213. Ibid, p. 120; (p. 123).
214. Ibid, p. 272; (p. 281).
215. Ibid, p. 356; (p. 370).
216. Ibid, p. 359; (p. 373).
217. Ibid, p. 29; (p. 28).
218. Ibid, p. 345; (p. 359).
219. Ibid, p. 9; (p. 7).
220. Ibid, p. 244; (p. 252).
221. Ibid, p. 168; (p. 173).
222. Ibid, p. 167; (p. 172).
223. Ibid, p. 327; (p. 340).
224. Ibid, p. 461; (p. 480).
225. Ibid, p. 462; (p. 481).
226. Ibid, p. 486; (p. 506).
227. From Hans Egon Holthusen, *Die Welt ohne Transzendenz: Eine Studie zu Thomas Manns "Dr. Faustus" und seine Nebenschriften* (Hamburg, Second edition, 1954), p. 68.
228. Ibid, p. 489; (p. 509).
229. Ibid, p. 471; (p. 490).
230. Mann's letter of 7 June 1954 is republished in *The Letters of Thomas Mann*, selected and translated by Richard and Clara Winston (Harmondsworth, 1975), pp. 464–467 (p. 465).
231. See his letter to Ida Herz quoted in Hans Bürgin and Hans-Otto Mayer, *Thomas Mann: A Chronicle of his Life* (Alabama, 1969), pp. 248–249.
232. The first published part concluded with the suicide of Krull's father at the end of Part One, Chapter Nine in 1922. By 1937 Mann had added further sections up to and including Part Two, Chapter Four.
233. Thomas Mann, *A Sketch of My Life*, translated from the German by H. T. Lowe-Porter (New York, 1970), p. 43.

234. Thomas Mann, *Confessions of Felix Krull: Confidence Man* (Penguin edition, Harmondsworth, 1958), p. 5. For the German source, see Thomas Mann, *Die Bekenntnisse des Hochstaplers Felix Krull* (Fischer Taschenbuch, Frankfurt am Main, 1965), p. 5. Subsequent references are to both editions.
235. Ibid, p. 229; (p. 200).
236. Ibid, p. 66; (p. 61).
237. Ibid, p. 20; (p. 19).
238. Ibid, p. 21; (p. 20).
239. Ibid, p. 28; (p. 26).
240. Ibid, p. 197; (p. 172).
241. Ibid, p. 229; (p. 199).
242. Ibid, p. 44; (p. 41).
243. Ibid, p. 103; (p. 92).
244. Ibid, p. 25; (p. 23).
245. Ibid, p. 39; (pp. 36–37).
246. Ibid, p. 172; (p. 151).
247. See the entry for 17 September 1918 in Thomas Mann, *Diaries for 1918–1939*, translated from the German by Richard and Clara Winston, selection and foreword by Hermann Kesten (New York, 1982), pp. 5–6 (p. 6).
248. *The Confessions of Felix Krull*, p. 322; (p. 279).
249. Ibid, p. 244; (p. 212).
250. Ibid, p. 199; (p. 174).
251. Tony Tanner, *City of Words: American Fiction, 1950–1970* (London, 1971), p. 31.
252. *The Confessions of Felix Krull*, p. 231; (p. 201).
253. Ibid, p. 205; (p. 179).
254. Ibid, p. 75; (p. 68).
255. Ibid, p. 73; (p. 66).
256. Ibid, p. 60; (p. 56).
257. Ibid, p. 347; (p. 300).
258. See Mann's letter to Michael Ott of 20 May 1948, republished in *Dichter über ihre Dichtungen*, Volume VI/1, *Thomas Mann, Part I: 1889–1917*, edited by Hans Wysling, with Marianne Fischer (Passau, 1975), pp. 570–571 (p. 571).
259. A selection of his essays are available in Thomas Mann, *Essays of Three Decades*, translated from the German by H. T. Lowe-Porter (New York, 1971).

# Select Bibliography

## I  PUBLICATIONS BY THOMAS MANN

The standard editions of Mann's work in German are the *Gesammelte Werke*, 13 vols (Fischer, Frankfurt am Main, 1960) and (in paperback) the 'Fischer Taschenbuchausgabe', *Werke*, 12 vols (Frankfurt am Main, 1967). In English, Penguin publish all the major works, including his letters (see below) and his extensive essay on Wagner, *Pro and Contra Wagner*. Other important works by Mann in English include: *Reflections of a Nonpolitical Man*, translated, and with an introduction, by Walter D. Morris (New York, 1983); *A Sketch of My Life*, translated by H. T. Lowe-Porter (New York, 1970) (originally published in German in 1930); *Essays of Three Decades*, translated from the German by H. T. Lowe-Porter (London, 1947); and *Thomas Mann's Addresses, delivered at the Library of Congress, 1942–1949* (Washington, 1963), which include 'The War and the Future' and 'Germany and the Germans'. Of less consequence but frequently insightful are the numerous interviews that Mann gave, and a selection has been collected in Volker Hansen and Gert Heine (eds), *Frage und Antwort: Interviews mit Thomas Mann, 1909–1955* (Hamburg, 1983).

*The Letters of Thomas Mann*, selected and translated by Richard and Clara Winston (Harmondsworth, 1975), and his *Diaries for 1918–1939*, translated from the German by Richard and Clara Winston (New York, 1982) are indispensable sources of information about his life and art. Mann's views on his own writings have been collected in *Dichter über ihre Dichtungen*, Volume 14, *Thomas Mann, Part I: 1889–1917* and *Part II: 1918–1943*, edited by Hans Wysling with Marianne Fischer (Passau, 1975).

## II  SELECTED SECONDARY PUBLICATIONS

Mann has been well served by a number of excellent general studies of his work, many in English. Foremost amongst the latter is T. J. Reed's *Thomas Mann: The Uses of Tradition* (Oxford, 1974), which offers not only a reliable reading of the individual texts of Mann's oeuvre, but also a wealth of information regarding the background and the genesis of his fiction. More speculative in nature but highly thoughtful are: Erich Heller, *The Ironic German: A Study of Thomas Mann* (London 1958), second edition 1973, and R. J. Hollingdale's *Thomas Mann: A Critical Study* (Lewisburg, 1971), who helpfully groups his study around such central Mannian concepts as 'Irony', 'Decadence', 'Myth' and 'Sickness'. Georg Lukács is the most perceptive of the Marxist critics who have written about Mann. His *Essays on Thomas Mann* (London, 1964) discuss Mann within the intellectual and political context of his times. Many interesting insights into Mann's oeuvre are provided by briefer introductions, such as R. Hinton Thomas's *Thomas Mann: The Mediation of Art* (Oxford, 1956), Andrew White's *Thomas Mann* (Edinburgh, 1965), Ignace Feuerlicht's, *Thomas Mann* (New York, 1968) and (particularly) Martin Swales, *Thomas Mann: A Study* (London, 1980).

The extensive secondary literature on Mann has been reviewed by Hermann Kurzke, *Thomas Mann Forschung, 1969–1976: Ein kritischer Bericht* (Frankfurt am Main, 1977), and, more recently, by Volkmar Hansen, *Thomas Mann*, in the 'Sammlung Metzler' Series (Stuttgart, 1984). Finally, how Mann's contemporary friends and critics saw his work is well documented in Klaus Schröter (ed.), *Thomas Mann im Urteil seiner Zeit: Dokumente, 1891–1955* (Hamburg, 1961).

Owing to his premature death, Peter de Mendelssohn's biography of Mann did not get beyond the initial volume: *Der Zauberer: Das Leben des deutschen Schriftstellers Thomas Mann: Erster Teil, 1915–1918* (Frankfurt am Main, 1975). For the non-German speaking reader, Richard Winston covers the same period in his *Thoms Mann: The Making of an Artist, 1875–1911* (London, 1982). An overview of Mann's entire life is given by Klaus Schröter in his *Thomas Mann* (Hamburg, 1968) in the Rowohlt monograph series. Nigel Hamilton's *The Brothers Mann: The Lives of Heinrich and Thomas Mann, 1871–1950 and 1875–1955* (New Haven, 1979) provides a concise and interesting comparison of the lives of the two literary brothers. Finally, in the absence of a full-length biography of Mann, readers will find Hans Bürgin's and Hans-Otto Mayer's, *Thomas Mann: A Chronicle of his Life*, translated into English by Eugene Dobson (Alabama, 1969) indispensable.

*Buddenbrooks* has remained Mann's most popular novel, and has, consequently, attracted a number of in-depth studies accessible to student and general reader alike. Foremost amongst these are Jochen Vogt's, *Thomas Mann: "Buddenbrooks"* (Munich, 1983), and Hugh Ridley's, *Thomas Mann: Buddenbrooks* (Cambridge, 1987). Both cover the major themes of the novel and address themselves to techniques such as irony or the use of the *leit motif*. Herbert Lehnert's essay on *Buddenbrooks* in Paul Lützeler (ed.), *Deutsche Romane des 20. Jahrhunderts: Neue Interpretationen* (Frankfurt am Main, 1983), pp. 31–49, is an excellent all-round introduction to the novel, as is Henry Hatfield's 'Thomas Mann's *Buddenbrooks*: The World of the Father', in Henry Hatfield (ed.), *Thomas Mann: A Collection of Criticial Essays* (New York, 1964), pp. 10–21.

Mann's early short stories have received disappointingly little attention. Erdmann Neumeister's *Thomas Manns frühe Erzählungen: Der Jugendstil als Kunstform im frühen Werk* (Bonn, 1977) offers many insights, but many readers will find its approach offputting. Helmut Haug focuses upon the nature of artistic alienation in his *Erkenntnisekel: Zum frühen Werk Thomas Manns* (Tübingen, 1969). Frank W. Young's *Montage and Motif in Thomas Manns 'Tristan'* (Bonn, 1975) offers an exhausting study of the influence of Wagner on that *Novelle*. A seminal reading of *Tonio Kröger* is provided by E. M.

Wilkinson in her 'Tonio Kröger: An Interpretation', in Hatfield (ed.), op. cit., pp. 22–34. Readers will also find much useful information in Hans Rudolf Vaget's, *Thomas Mann: Kommentar zu sämtlichen Erzählungen* (Winkler, 1984).

Peter Heller discusses *Death in Venice* in the context of Mann's early preoccupation with the figure of the artist in *'Der Tod in Venedig* und Thomas Manns Grudmotive', in Hans Schulte and Gerald Chapple (eds), *Thomas Mann: Ein Kolloquium* (Bonn, 1978), pp. 35–83. Quite indispensable are the editions of the novella prepared by T. J. Reed with introduction and notes, in English (Oxford, 1971) and in German (Munich, 1983). An excellent introduction to the *Death in Venice* is provided by Heinz Gockel's essay, 'Aschenbachs Tod in Venedig' in a volume of the excellent 'Sammlung Profile' series edited by Rudolf Wolff, *Thomas Mann: Erzählungen und Novellen* (Bonn, 1984), pp. 27–41.

Thomas Mann called *The Magic Mountain* a 'parody of the *Bildungsroman*', and the status of the novel within that genre has been examined in detail by Hermann J. Weigand in his seminal study, *The Magic Mountain: A Study of Thomas Mann's Novel "Der Zauberberg"* (Chapel Hill, 1965), and more recently by Michael Beddow in his *The Fiction of Humanity: Studies in the 'Bildungsroman' from Wieland to Thomas Mann* (Cambridge, 1982), pp. 230–286, and Martin Swales, *The German Bildungsroman from Wieland to Hesse* (Princeton, 1978), pp. 105–128. The genesis of the novel is outlined in Jens Rieckmann, *"Der Zauberberg": Eine geistige Autobiographie Thomas Mann* (Stuttgart 1977), and in Heinz Sa025ereßig, *Die Entstehung des Romans "Der Zauberberg": Zwei Essays und eine Dokumentation* (Biberch an der Riss, 1965). Ulrich Karthaus's essay on *Der Zauberberg* in Paul Lützeler (ed.), *Deutsche Romane des 20. Jahrhunderts: Neue Interpretationen* (Frankfurt am Main, 1983), pp. 95–109 provides a useful introduction to the novel.

The novella *Mario and the Magician* seems to have been rediscovered as a major text in the past decade. Gert Sautermeister offers a full-length study of the story in his *Thomas Mann: Mario und der Zauberer* (Munich, 1981) in Fink's 'Text und Geschichte' series. The political dimension of the story is well discussed by Eugene Lunn, 'Tales of Liberal Disquiet: Thomas Mann's Mario and the Magician and Interpretations of Fascism', *Literature and History*, 11 (1985) 77–100. Anthony Grenville in his 'Idealism versus Materialism in the Representation of History in Literature: The Dictator Figure in Thomas Mann's "Mario und der Zauberer" and Brecht's "Der aufhaltsame Aufstieg des Arturo Ui"', *Journal of European Studies*, 17 (1987), 77–105 offers an interesting point of comparison between the Marxist Brecht and the non-Marxist Thomas Mann, whilst, by focusing upon the role of the narrator, Alan Bance arrives at a somewhat more critical reading of the political content of the story in his 'The Narrator in Thomas Mann's "Mario und der Zauberer"', *The Modern Language Review*, 82 (1987), 382–398. The role of the reader (who is addressed by the narrator in an act of complicity throughout the story) is discussed in Grant F. Leneaux, '"Mario und der Zauberer": The Narration of Seduction or the Seduction of Narration?', *Orbis Litterarum*, 40 (1985), 327–47.

The Joseph novel tetralogy has been particularly well served by Mann scholars. Notable studies include Käte Hamburger's most recent study, *Thomas Manns biblisches Werk: Der Joseph-Roman, die Moses-Erzählung, 'das Gesetz'* (Munich, 1981); Dietmar Mieth, *Epik und Ethik: Eine theologischethische*

*Interpretation der Josephromane Thomas Manns* (Tübingen, 1976); and Willy R. Berger, *Die mythologischen Motive in Thomas Manns Roman 'Joseph and seine Brüder'* (Vienna, 1971), which importantly establishes many of the non-Christian myths that exist behind Thomas Mann's use of the Old Testament story. Henry Hatfield approaches the same aspect from a rather different angle in his essay 'Myth versus Secularism: Religion in Thomas Mann's Joseph', in Inta M. Ezergailis (ed.), *Critical Essays on Thomas Mann* (Massachusetts, 1988), pp. 115–23.

The two volumes by Rudolf Wolff (ed.), *Thomas Manns Docktor Faustus und die Wirkung* (Bonn, 1983), in the 'Sammlung Profile' series brings together excellent essays by Georg Lukács, Käte Hamburger, Kurt Sontheimer and Paul Gerhard Klussman on Thomas Mann's use of the Faust myth and the status of the novel as an historical novel or *Zeitroman*. This is also the focus of Hans Wisskirchen's thoughtful study, *Zeitgeschichte im Roman: Zu Thomas Manns 'Zauberberg' und 'Doktor Faustus'* (Francke, 1986). For non-German readers, the essays by J. P. Stern, 'History and Allegory in Thomas Mann's Doctor Faustus', (Inaugural Lecture, University College, London, 1973), and T. J. Reed, 'The Writer as Historian of his Time', *Modern Language Review* (1976), 82–96 provide stimulating introductions. Mann's detailed use of music as a vehicle for his political allegory are well discussed by Patrick Carnegg in his, *Faust as Musician: A Study of Thomas Mann's Novel 'Doctor Faustus'* (London, 1973), whilst the sources and genesis of the novel are exhaustively researched in Gunilla Bergtsen, *Thomas Mann's 'Doctor Faustus': The Sources and Structure of the Novel* (Chicago, 1969), and Lieselotte Voss, *Die Entstehung von Thomas Manns Roman 'Doktor Faustus': Dargestellt anhand von unveröffentlichen Vorarbeiten* (Tübingen, 1975).

The most comprehensive account of *The Confessions of Felix Krull: Confidence Man* is Hans Wysling's *Narzissmus und illusionäre Existenzform: Zu Bekenntnissen des Hochstaplers Felix Krull* (Bern and Munich, 1982), which not only offers an account of the many facets of Thomas Mann's great picaresque novel but includes important primary materials from the Mann Archive in Zurich. A similar range of themes is covered in a much shorter space by Guido Stein in his *Thomas Mann: Bekenntnissen des Hochstaplers Felix Krull Künstler und Komödiant* (Paderborn, 1984), in the Schöningh 'Modellanalysen' Series. In English, Robert B. Heilman's essay, 'Variations on the Picaresque', in Hatfield (ed.), op. cit., pp. 133–54, offers a good starting point. Claus Sommerhage's *Eros und Poesie: Über das Erotische im Werk Thomas Manns* (Bonn, 1983) discusses the role of the erotic in Mann's entire oeuvre.

# Index